# BECOMING a KNEW YOU

## A GUIDE TO LEARNING HOW YOUR PAST CAN INFORM YOUR PRESENT

### KIARA LUNA, LMHC

Paperback ISBN: 978-1-63616-093-1
Hardcover ISBN: 978-1-63616-094-8
eBook ISBN: 978-1-63616-095-5

Published By Opportune Independent Publishing Co.
Edited by Speak Write Play, LLC
Image credit to Ольга Погорелова

Printed in the United States of America
For permission requests, email the author with the subject line as "Attention: Permissions Coordinator" to the email address below:

Info@opportunepublishing.com

# DEDICATION

I dedicate this book to all the individuals out there looking for answers, understanding, and insight as to why they are the way they are.

I dedicate this book to couples looking for understanding on what shows up in their relationships and how to work through those things.

Finally, I dedicate this book to my community, culture, and loving family. We all need so much healing and understanding about how our past experiences shape us.

# CONTENTS

# ACKNOWLEDGMENTS

First, I want to thank God because, without him, this would have never happened.

Thank you to my family and closest friends for their constant motivation and for being my biggest fans. This journey has not been easy, and it would have never been possible without my family's constant support, the powerful women I have met throughout my career, and the team behind executing this book. I appreciate you all so much!!

Finally, a special thank you to my husband and children for their patience, love, and compassion throughout my journey!

Thank you all for believing in me and seeing things I could not see in myself at times!

# FOR HER

*This section is dedicated to all women looking for a deeper understanding.*

Because you are women, people will force their ideas and expectations on you. Don't live in the shadows of what people project onto you. Make your own choices based on your own wisdom.

Note: This section can also pertain to men.

# INTRODUCTION

As I became older, I realized how much people go around the world hurting others due to their traumas and unhealed wounds. A lot of us walk through life not aware of the pain and suffering we cause others. Without realizing it, we treat other people the same exact way we were treated during childhood. We have so many negative memories suppressed because we choose to avoid the pain. If there is one thing that I have learned through life experiences and my work, it is that the pain will always catch up to you and be projected onto those around you.

So, why did I write this book? I wrote *Becoming a Knew You* because I believe that the world would be a better place if all individuals had more self-awareness about their childhood experiences and how those experiences play a role in their lives today. I believe that if you increase your awareness about your own patterns of behaviors, you can break through generational traumas. I believe that if you were to focus on your history, which made you who you are today, and gain awareness of your maladaptive coping behaviors, you would be able to develop better relationships, not only with others but also with yourself!

In this book, you will notice that I ask you to think back to your childhood often; this will help you uncover deeply held feelings and experiences you have probably never linked to current behaviors, triggers, emotions, and/or thoughts.

Let the healing begin!

# 1 LOW SELF-ESTEEM

*YOU, YOURSELF, AS MUCH AS ANYBODY IN THE ENTIRE UNIVERSE, DESERVE YOUR LOVE AND AFFECTION.*

—BUDDHA

Many different types of experiences may lead to low self-esteem. Some of them are the following: making comparisons, having emotionally distant parents, being bullied, feeling rejected because of the way you look, coming from a critical and judgmental home, and feeling the pressure to conform to societal beauty standards.

Now, I would like you to take some time to ask and answer the following questions:
How was I described growing up?
How did my parents and/or caretakers describe me?
How did they make me feel?
What is the first memory I can recall of me adapting negative self-talk?
What are my current thoughts about myself?
When I look at myself in the mirror, what do I see?

There may be many reasons why you see what you see in the mirror. Perhaps, in your environment, you constantly felt judged and/or criticized by your parents and/or caretakers. Maybe you were constantly compared to others. In your environment, maybe your family members thought love was shown by them being critical and harsh to you, so pointing out your "imperfections" was the way to motivate you to change them. But their words made you feel smaller, less than, inferior, and not good enough. In order to cope with this, you learned early on to hide parts of yourself that showed those "imperfections" because, like most children, you just wanted to feel accepted and loved.

As time passed, you began to become self-critical and adapted the language you had heard your parents and/or caretakers use to refer to you. Without realizing it, your confidence level was impacted, and you no longer saw yourself in a positive light. In fact, you believed every negative word and began feeding your soul with them. I mean, it makes sense. At some point, you had to take control of other people making you feel the way they did by saying those things to yourself. Now, when others criticize you, you might think, *You are not saying anything I don't already know or feel*, which makes you believe you are unbothered by their words.

There also might have been times when you attempted to speak your mind, share your ideas, or offer your opinions but were met with degrading language like "that is stupid," "no one thinks like that," or "you are an idiot for thinking this way." As time passed, these statements taught you that your opinions did not matter, and you had nothing good to offer. As a result, you decided to no longer share your inner thoughts with others. You now have difficulty speaking your truth, speaking up, and sharing your ideas because you are afraid of being rejected or ridiculed. Instead of accepting this, we tend to give ourselves personality traits, such as being "shy," to describe our maladaptive coping behavior.

Also, be aware of the impact of certain teachers from your childhood. I remember receiving a lot of negative feedback from some of my high school teachers because of their own frustrations from dealing with me. A comment made by one teacher has always stuck with me. The teacher said, "You would never be anything in life." That comment hit me harder than she would ever know. Even though the comment made me really upset, I acted as if it did not faze me and just shrugged my shoulders to give her the impression that I did not care about what she said. Every time I failed an exam or did not do well enough, her voice got louder and louder in my head. That is, until the day I decided to silence her by telling myself that her words would not become my destiny, taking control of the external voice that I had made internal. Since not many around me fed me with what I needed during my teenage years, I began to feed myself. I had no idea the impact this action was going to have at that time, but when I look back now as an adult and a therapist, I see how I saved myself because of that single decision.

As an adult, you may have difficulties feeling good about yourself, your decisions, your relationships, and where you are in life. You might find yourself seeking external validation in order to feel good about yourself. At some point, you depend on how others view you because you know you cannot rely on how you see yourself, so you begin to measure your success, beauty, and standards by how others see them. Due to feeling constantly rejected, invalidated, and unlovable, you now desperately look for ways to fit in, doing so at the expense of who you truly are. You begin to change aspects of your life to conform to others' opinions or expectations. You are primarily dependent on the reactions and responses of other people rather than your own natural inclinations, so you search to receive their approval, attention, and admiration. Constantly looking for ways to fit in leads you to making inauthentic decisions about your life, looking for something you are not giving yourself.

At times, you might feel like the people who come into your life are as harsh as your parents and/or caretakers, which leads you to believe that you don't deserve love and compassion. You find yourself constantly being triggered and do not understand why. The reality is that you have grown up without compassion and empathy, so you had to learn ways of adapting to such an environment to fit in. That kind of environment is all you know; it is the environment you have grown to become comfortable in. Also, you might have learned that you should not expect compassion from others, so you enter into relationships devoid of love and compassion but become triggered because your heart knows something is not right.

There also might be difficulties recognizing what you can do to help yourself; the thought that you could ever feel better or differently feels foreign or impossible. The truth is, we were not born hating ourselves; this is a learned behavior. And just like it is learned, it can also be unlearned. It is not an easy process, but it's doable. I am here to help you begin the process. What if I told you that you have control and can make changes to help increase your self-esteem today? Would you believe me? What if I told you that by changing your patterns of behaviors, thought processes, and self-talk, you can, slowly but surely, begin to see things differently for yourself? Would you believe me? I want you to know that it is all possible. I know this might sound like a cliché, but anything that we put our minds to is possible. We just have to want it for ourselves. The only reason why you believe all those negative things about yourself is because you have done a great job of consistently speaking negatively to yourself. What do you think would happen if you replaced those negative thoughts with positive ones? That is right, you would begin to believe them. I know it may be hard to accept that this is even possible right now, but I just need you to want to change.

I have helped thousands of women build their self-esteem; find their voices; redefine their lives; take control over their wants, needs, and desires; and silence the inner critical voices they have developed as they learned that those voices no longer served them. You can do the same. You are no longer a powerless child; you are an adult who gets to make decisions about how you want your life to be moving forward. No one else has control over who you want to really become. You have grown up to believe that you must pretend to fit in or be liked. But the reality is that when we don't live up to who we are—when we are not authentically ourselves or hide parts of ourselves—we attract people who stay for who we are not. More often than not, those are not satisfying relationships.

You want people who love you and want to be around you for who you truly are. Whoever loves you and wants to be in your life will stay no matter what. Yes, as you make changes in your life people will also choose to walk away; that is okay. Some people are only meant to be part of our lives for a temporary time; they were supposed to come into our lives to teach us something about the world or ourselves. My point is, some people will stay, and some people will go. At the end of the day, you want whoever stays for who you are, not who you are not; pretending can be exhausting.

You might be thinking, *This sounds great, Kiara, but where do I begin?* Well, you are going to begin this process by gaining insight into your boundaries.

# Boundaries

According to an article written by Sam Blum, boundaries are the rules, limitations, and expectations you set for yourself within your relationships. If you have healthy boundaries, it means you can say "no" to others when you want to without feeling guilt or remorse.[1] It also means "you are comfortable opening yourself up to intimacy and close relationships". Being aware of your boundaries helps you make decisions you are comfortable with in life. Boundaries should be based on your values, morals, and the things that are important to you. Your boundaries are unique, which means that they might not always align with others. This makes it difficult for many to begin to establish boundaries because they fear losing the individuals they are close to. But let me ask you this, if the people who are close to you do not respect your boundaries and what you stand for, what does that mean to you?

He went on to explain that there are three different types of boundaries: rigid, porous, and healthy. When people have rigid boundaries, the chances they would ask for help are slim. They may also seem detached and emotionally disconnected, even within their intimate relationship being that they may experience difficulties being vulnerable and opening up to others. People with rigid boundaries might not have many close friends as they want to avoid any possibility of rejection and may behave in ways that is perceived as secretive as they can be very overprotective of their personal information. People with porous boundaries might overshare too many personal details about their lives with others. They at times may accept disrespect from others due to fear of abandonment. They also may depend on the opinions and validation of others often and face difficulties refusing to do the requests of others as they fear they can possibly be rejected if they do not comply. People with healthy boundaries are able to accept "no" for an answer; stick to their beliefs in difficult situations; value their own opinions; typically seek support and share information appropriately; and are able to express their needs, wants, and desires. Now, as you read about the different types of boundaries

1      Blum, Sam. "The Five Types of Personal Boundaries (and How to Set Them)." Lifehacker. Last modified July 23, 2021. https://lifehacker.com/the-five-types-of-personal-boundaries-and-how-to-set-t-1847349639.

and characteristics, you might have found that you have a little bit of everything or that you fit one type more than another. Some people might have a mixture of different types of boundaries, and that's okay. It's important to decide which environments are appropriate for you to exhibit porous, rigid, and healthy boundaries. While you may feel comfortable oversharing in your intimate relationships, it might not be appropriate to do the same at your workplace.

*I highly recommend that you take some time to write down your values and expectations in the following areas to begin working on establishing boundaries.*

Physical boundaries pertaining to physical touch:

_____

_____

Material boundaries pertaining to possessions and money:

_____

_____

Intellectual boundaries pertaining to your thoughts, ideas, and the respect you expect from others:

_____

_____

Emotional boundaries relating to your feelings being respected:

_____

_____

Sexual boundaries referring to the emotional, physical, and intellectual aspects of your sexual life:

_____

_____

Time boundaries referring to how you allow others to use your time:

_____

_____

# Exercise

What does an invasion of my space look like? What does it look like when someone invades my space?

_____

_____

It seems like people are always borrowing money from me. What does this mean to me? How does lending material things currently impact me?

_____

_____

What does it look like when I share my ideas and/or thoughts and get shut down? How will I begin to express my discomfort when I am met with criticism and/or judgment?

_____

_____

Who in my life currently makes me feel less than, and how can I have a conversation about this with them?

_____

_____

How much do I share about my feelings and with whom? What course of action do I want to take when I constantly feel belittled, criticized, or invalidated by the individuals in my life?

_____

_____

What sexual boundaries have I set with my intimate partner(s)?

_____

_____

How do I want to address when I am not okay with something?

_____

_____

What does my time mean to me? How do I want to spend my time?

_____

_____

How do I want to approach situations in which I feel my time being taken advantage of?

_____

_____

What boundaries do I need to set for myself? How do I want to exhibit or express them?

_____

_____

What has been my experience in setting boundaries? What challenges have I faced in trying to establish boundaries? Have I attempted to establish boundaries but stopped because of other people's responses?

_____

_____

All these questions might sound scary, and you might feel like implementing your responses might be challenging. It will be challenging. As I mentioned before, the process is difficult, but I assure you that by it will get easier with consistent practice. You will learn your limits and how to be assertive; others will learn to provide you with what you show them you deserve.

## How does low self-esteem show up in intimate relationships?

Being in a relationship is complicated, especially when you do not feel secure. This can bring up a mixture of feelings that can lead you to behave in ways that destroy your relationship. As a result of having low confidence, you might seek validation and reassurance from your partner often. There might also be an expectation that there is someone better out there in the world, and this statement might come up in arguments. Your partner might tell you that you are beautiful, but you may have difficulty believing the compliment is true because you do not feel the same way about yourself. Every time you hear it, you question your partner's words, which becomes frustrating. Because you always doubt your partner's intentions, your partner may stop giving you compliments, which would then result in you proving your underlying negative belief that you are "not good enough." I want you to understand that our underlying beliefs drive us to only see things that prove them to be correct. It is difficult to look for the opposite of what we believe in; no one likes to be proven wrong. This is why finding out our underlying beliefs and how we truly feel about ourselves is so important. Understanding your underlying beliefs allows you to discover the areas you need to work on and challenge in order to change.

Now, I know you want to improve in this area, so I have a secret to help with this and information on the most important relationship you have to strengthen first. In order to be able to improve in this area, you must first work on the relationship you have developed with yourself. Again, *you* must strengthen the relationship you have with *yourself*. We expect other people to give us what we do not give ourselves: compassion, validation, affirmations, love, etc. How come we expect others to treat us differently than how we treat ourselves? Just like we have to work on our relationships with other people—family, friends, coworkers, intimate partners, God, or any spiritual figure you may believe in—we must also work on the relationship we have developed with ourselves. So, what type of relationship do you have with yourself?

# Begin to build your relationship with yourself by:

- Identifying your wins—no matter how small you might consider them to be

- Highlighting your positive qualities

- Speaking to yourself with respect, love, and kindness

- Writing down things you are thankful for daily

- Being patient with yourself and the process

- Allowing yourself to feel and heal

## *Challenging negative self-talk and thoughts*

Poor self-esteem is often a result of irrational negative thoughts. You can receive multiple compliments a day, but when you have low self-esteem, it only takes one negative criticism to make you feel like you are not enough. That negative feedback, more often than not, then dictates how you feel about yourself entirely. This exercise will help you challenge yourself and those irrational thoughts to become more balanced and logical. This is a method I use when implementing cognitive behavioral interventions.[2]

**If we can change our thoughts, we can change our lives. Remember, you are in control now. You have the power!**

| | |
|---|---|
| What happened: | |
| What was my first Thought: | |
| Emotions I felt: | |
| Evidence for my automatic thought: | |
| Evidence against my automatic thought: | |

---

2     25 CBT techniques and worksheets for cognitive behavioral therapy. PositivePsychology.com. (2022, January 26), from https://positivepsychology.com/cbt-cognitive-behavioral-therapy-techniques-worksheets/

# How would I revise my automatic thought to make it more realistic?

# 2 TRUST ISSUES

*BEING TRUTHFUL TO YOURSELF AND OTHERS IS ONE OF THE BEST GIFTS YOU CAN GIVE YOURSELF.*

## *How much do you trust yourself?*

Trust is one of the most important components in relationships, yet it can be one of the most difficult to cultivate and maintain, even with ourselves. Trust issues can also be overall feelings you have due to childhood experiences. Some of us are products of divorced parents, violent environments, emotional or physical childhood abuse, dysfunctional family dynamics, substance use, the child welfare system, or adoption. The number one thing we needed as children was to feel protected, loved, and cared for; unfortunately, having grown up in the environments previously mentioned, it may be difficult to trust anyone.

If you grew up in an environment where you constantly witnessed your mother getting hurt by your father's actions, the chances of you trusting that your intimate partner has your best interest at heart is difficult. If you grew up in an environment where you could not speak your mind about how you felt because you were always met with anger and frustration, one maladaptive coping skill you might have adapted early on was to suppress those parts of yourself by no longer verbalizing how you felt. As a result of growing up in toxic and unhealthy environments, we began to develop ways to relate to the world in order to fit in. We began to hide parts of ourselves because we believed those parts were not good. We also did it because, as children, all we wanted was to feel accepted by our parents and caretakers. As we grew older, we started to relate to others with caution and hypervigilance. While we may develop relationships with others, we might not feel as connected because there are parts of ourselves that we do not show. In fact, there is a high possibility that you might not feel connected to yourself at times either. This typically happens because you might not be aware of those parts of yourself that you put away as a child to adapt. Also, we find comfort in these environments, even right now. Remember that comfort is important for us as human. So, if all your life you've been exposed to chaos, that is what you will almost always place yourself in; that is what you are comfortable and know how to survive in.

Now, as an adult, you have trouble building relationships because you have set rigid boundaries within all relationships, including the one you have with yourself. Due to these trust issues, you question if anyone has your best interest at heart; you expect to be played or receive the short end of the stick. You think, *Well, why would anyone want to stay? I grew up witnessing everyone leave out of my life.* These limited beliefs typically take over your relationships, so you only depend on yourself because that is exactly what you had to do as a child. You had to depend on yourself for food, to feel protected, and to self-soothe. You might have even been responsible for taking care of others early in life. As a child, you learned to be reliable because you had to. So, as an adult, you are a reliable person; anyone can count on you for anything, even at the expense of your own gratification at times.

There are many ways to trust others. You can trust someone will always be there for you to protect you emotionally, financially, etc. As an adult, trust issues show up in your relationship as you begin to notice that your partner is behaving suspiciously or doing things that lead you to believe that they are lying or being unfaithful. You start to explore whether your suspicions are correct by checking your partner's phone and social media accounts, eavesdropping on phone calls, questioning their whereabouts or new relationships, and constantly scanning for evidence of disloyalty.

I am going to let you in another secret because, as I mentioned earlier, this is for people who are ready to work on themselves and identify their patterns of behaviors in order to change. When we engage in behaviors that provide us with temporary relief, we create a pattern of behavior to obtain that relief more often because it feels enjoyable momentarily; however, this behavior keeps the underlying fear intact and extends it. For example, you might think your partner is cheating, so you become an FBI agent and begin to search for evidence to prove that your theory is true. After looking through all their devices, you realize that your partner is not being unfaithful. Finding that out gives you peace of mind, but this relief lasts only until the next time when your partner does something that triggers your suspicions. The pattern of behavior in this case is checking the phone or social media. This becomes an unhealthy cycle that continues to play out.

You might know deep down in your heart that your partner is not being disloyal. Your partner has pure intentions, but it is difficult to believe that you have truly found someone who sincerely cares for you, is willing to stay and protect you, and loves you as deeply as they can because all of your past experiences. You might even begin to doubt the fact that your partner is open with you about their whereabouts, friends, phone, social media, and life in general. You may even see a red flag in that.

I can absolutely relate to the scenario I just presented; trusting others, especially romantic partners, was a challenge I had to learn to overcome for the betterment of my relationship and myself. I grew up around men who were disloyal to the women in their lives, and this was also part of my own family dynamic. I learned that, at the end of the day, I had to work on myself and understand that I was no longer a child looking to be protected emotionally; I was now an adult looking to feel protected within my own self. I worked on my confidence and identified what I brought to the table, realizing that there was no need for me to worry because the actions of others were a projection of who they are, not what I lacked. I took a step back to remind myself that I was worthy of all the good that came my way— that I deserved it. I also repeatedly reminded myself that I was good enough, and whoever did not see that value in me, did not deserve to be in my circle. When I came to this conclusion, my life changed. I blossomed and grew, and so did all my relationships.

I know trusting others is hard, so—as always—I go back to developing a trusting relationship with yourself. If you can trust yourself in all the ways you seek trust in others, you will realize that trusting other people who earn that trust is easier for you. But the work must first begin with you. Trust that you can provide yourself with care, unconditional love, protection, gratitude, respect, honesty, and transparency. Be true to who you are. Look within and accept your flaws. We are imperfect human beings, so we are always going to have areas that need improvement. Identify those areas and be vulnerable with yourself in order to heal through those deep childhood wounds. You deserve to live the fulfilled life you desire.

# Dig Deeper - TRUST

What keeps me from trusting myself and/or others?

_____

_____

What childhood experiences have led me to having trust issues?

_____

_____

What can I begin to do differently today to allow myself to trust?

_____

_____

What events and/or incidents typically trigger me to become distrustful?

_____

_____

What areas of my life can I trust myself in more?

_____

_____

What emotions do I experience when I feel betrayed?

_____

_____

How do I want to move forward if someone does not provide me with what I need while I am in the healing process of developing trust?

_____

_____

## *Tips to develop self-trust and trust for others*

Identify the areas where you have to develop self-trust.

Be vulnerable with yourself about how you feel.

Be vulnerable with others about the actions, if any, they might be exhibiting that lead you to distrusting them.

Exercise vulnerability with others about how past experiences have developed your overall distrustful character.

Let yourself feel the emotions flow through yourself and your body.

Monitor your emotions when you don't trust yourself and challenge negative thoughts.

Be true to yourself and others about what you need.

Commit to yourself, others, and the process.

Take your time to make decisions.

Be patient because the process takes time.

# 3

## PEOPLE-PLEASING

*WHEN YOU SAY 'YES' TO OTHERS, MAKE SURE IT'S NOT AT THE EXPENSE OF YOUR OWN GRATIFICATION.*

Growing up in a home where you constantly felt like you had to cater to others in order to keep the peace can show up in ways you never imagined in your adulthood. People-pleasing is a symptom of overly pleasing others to earn their approval. You might engage in this behavior to avoid guilt from feeling selfish, prevent others from feeling pain, or avoid conflict. You also may display people-pleasing behaviors to maintain connections you think you might lose if you don't comply, which leads you to feeling taken advantage of or being resentful more often than not.

At some point, you might have felt powerless as a child, so to gain some control, you learned to locate your parent's happiness or unhappiness within yourself. Maybe you knew that if you did anything and everything for your mother to cheer her up, she would forget the pain she just experienced from her own toxic relationship and become happy. In turn, this made you happy because your mother was happy that you made her happy. As a result, you developed a source that fulfilled your need of feeling loved and experiencing happiness: pleasing others.

Perhaps in your childhood, you experienced your parents always having arguments. If there was any abuse in your environment, physical or verbal, you might have developed the trait of agreeableness in order to not trigger abusive behaviors in your caretakers. This was your defense mechanism to staying safe and protecting those around you. At an early age, you learned that always following the rules and being perfect was a way to avoid people being upset with you or rejecting you.

Along similar lines, you might have also learned that withholding the truth was a useful tool, meaning that you realized early on that lying and hiding your true feelings, thoughts, and emotions provided you with what you wanted most from your parents: love and affection. By lying, you were not met with disappointment and anger. So, as an adult, you typically withhold the truth, lie about things unnecessarily, and often feel empty at times. You now consistently lie in order to make others happy at the expense of you feeling fulfilled and happy. Some of the consequences with this maladaptive schema as an adult are losing those close to you, feeling disconnected from yourself and others, having a hard time maintaining meaningful relationships, and believing the stories you say about yourself in order to fit in.

People-pleasing is developed out of a fear of rejection or abandonment. If you grew up with emotionally unavailable parents and a lack of closeness and connection, you might have learned that being emotionally connected was a privilege rather than a need; you learned to fulfill that need and connection you were looking for by making others happy. Now, as an adult, you might be perceived as being "needy" and have difficulty connecting with your true self.

As a child, you might have found yourself looking for signs of discomfort in your caretakers. You may have tried hard to make your parents proud and happy all the time. Because you had no idea how to create a secure place where you felt loved and cared for, you began to adapt your parents' dreams and values in order to fit into their world and earn their love. At that point, you stopped being curious about yourself—who you were, what you liked, things in your world—and focused instead on what other people wanted you to be. You learned that being nice to others all the time secured you receiving love and care.

# People-pleasing in your relationships

You might often take the initiative in completing tasks for your partner in your relationship. You might even think, *If I don't complete it, it will not get done.* You do this because part of you is happy to finish the task, but the other part is upset because you bear the responsibility often and may not feel seen or noticed for your efforts. This leads to a build-up of resentment in your relationship because you continuously feel like you do so much, but your partner does not do enough. This is another way to feel like you are getting the short end of the stick.

Now, as an adult, you might find it difficult to set boundaries and limits. You find a lot of pleasure in helping others but might feel stuck in relationships where you give more than you receive, are always compromising more than others, and experience burnout for attempting to meet the personal and professional needs of others. While you might look back at your childhood and think you were attuned to your parents and caretakers, you may realize that there was no connection, and your emotional needs were not met. Individuals who engage in people-pleasing typically do not recognize that they continue to respond in the same manner to their own selves beyond childhood. They continue neglecting their own needs and desires to put others first. Because they learned that meeting their needs was not a priority growing up, they adapted this behavior as being "normal" and found ways to cope with it.

## *How can you work toward creating a healthier balance?*

Some adults who struggle with people-pleasing have a difficult time remembering instances when they experienced a lack of warmth or connection with their parents. They may only recall the loving moments, which can be confusing. Your parents might have been loving, caring, and emotionally available to you; however, there were also times when their affection was inconsistent. One day, they could have been loving, but they could have been distant, cold, and absent the next day. As a child, you had no idea what was going on or what you did, so you began to look for ways to get your loving parents back.

The first step toward creating a healthier balance is to recognize that you have people-pleasing tendencies. Then, examine the different ways those tendencies show up. Finally, make a list of boundaries you want to begin to set for yourself and your relationships. Also, make a list of tasks you typically take the initiative to complete for others. Be sure to include the ones you do for the household, as well as, if applicable, the ones that directly benefit your partner exclusively. After, prepare to have a conversation with your partner about your new findings. You can say, "I have noticed I typically engage in people-pleasing activities to avoid rejection or abandonment," "I have realized how much I am scared to lose you, and because of that, I put so much pressure on myself," or "I take on so much out of fear, which then leads me to feel resentful. I no longer want to do this and need your help to begin making changes." Take accountability for your behaviors and feelings, then ask for help with this process. Speaking up to your partner will bring clarity, connection, vulnerability, and understanding. These are some of the steps to get you started within your relationship to begin making positive changes and setting boundaries.

Now that you have an idea of some of the reasons why you might develop people-pleasing behaviors, let's talk about how this can impact you.

## The impact of people-pleasing:

**Low self-esteem:** You may not feel good about or tend to be critical of yourself.

**Sense of feeling burnout:** You always give more than you should in all aspects of your life, which typically leaves you with little to no time for yourself.

**Lack of authenticity:** People-pleasers often hide their true selves, as well as their needs and desires, to accommodate others. This can result in feeling lost and not knowing who you really are because you have been out of touch with yourself.

**Involvement in dissatisfying relationships:** In some relationships, you may feel like you are always giving more. Since this is your natural nature, people might not realize that you may feel taken advantage of. Because your efforts might not be appreciated as expected at times, you may begin to feel taken for granted.

**Loneliness:** While people-pleasers are often well-liked by others because they are so busy pleasing others, they are typically loved and appreciated for what they do for others rather than for who they are as individuals.

**Agreeableness:** People-pleasers are agreeable and have difficulty saying "no" to others. Because they are so agreeable with requests, they often stretch themselves too thin.

Helping others and those you love is a kind act, and when this is done with balance, it is healthy and good for your soul. Issues arise when you give the same privileges to everyone in your life, leaving you with no time for yourself. Remember, this was a maladaptive coping skill developed to help you feel secure and loved as a child. As I mentioned before, at a certain point, you stopped being concerned about yourself and began to be concerned about other people's needs. It makes total sense that you did this. The reality is that you *deserved* to be loved without losing yourself for it.

I am sorry you felt you had to *earn* the love you deserved to be given as a child. You learned that the best way to survive and fit into your environment was through meeting the needs of others, so now that you have identified that you have neglected your needs because that is what you thought was best, let's work on digging deeper to learn more about yourself and figure out ways to challenge these behaviors in order to heal and become your authentic self. This work will ultimately lead you to loving, fulfilling relationships where you will attract people for who you are, not what they want you to be.

## Exercise

How did my parents or caretakers meet my emotional needs as a child?

_____

_____

How did I seek to connect with my parents or caretakers?

_____

_____

What was my experience when looking to feel connected?

_____

_____

What did I decide to do to avoid feeling rejected by others?

_____

_____

Whose world did I decide to fit into to avoid pain?

_____

_____

How does people-pleasing show up for me now?

_____

_____

What price am I paying for engaging in people-pleasing behaviors?

_____

_____

How does being a people-pleaser impact me personally?

_____

_____

What changes do I want to make in my life?

_____

_____

What boundaries do I want to set?

_____

_____

What can I do today to begin my journey?

_____

_____

## *Tips to challenge people-pleasing behaviors*

Understand the history of how you developed people-pleasing behaviors.

Take small steps.

Tune into your needs and wants.

Prioritize your needs.

Explore your values.

Set boundaries.

Explore your emotions.

Work on your self-esteem.

Take your time to process requests made by others.

Avoid making excuses.

Always remember that relationships require give and take.

Communicate your needs.

Help when you want to help.

Do what makes you happy.

Practice awareness and mindfulness.

Practice saying "no."

# 4 SHAME

*SHAME SURROUNDS US EVERYWHERE, AND IT DOES NOT ALLOW US TO FULLY BE OUR TRUE SELVES.*

Shame is generally developed from experiences that occurred in our most vulnerable developmental years. While shame might have a different meaning for everyone, we may all agree that we do not feel good about who we are as people when shame is the reality that surrounds our worlds.

Growing up, you might have heard your parents often describe you in negative terms. Shame is typically rooted in the way we were spoken to as children and potentially followed by other traumatic experiences. When your parents described you using degrading language, your brain began to react in ways it typically does when you are in physical danger. This activated your fight-flight-freeze response. Flight is typically activated by shame, so you might have often felt like you wanted to become invisible or disappear. As a child, you could not just leave the room or walk out as your parent or caretaker was yelling at or speaking down to you. Instead, you developed maladaptive mechanisms to manage. In exploring ways to be invisible and not get hurt, you might have found some of the following maladaptive behaviors to cope:

**Social isolation:** By isolating yourself, you noticed that you did not have to deal with personal attacks.

**Avoidance:** You developed ways to avoid situations, whether that was by using your words or physical body.

**Pleasing others:** You noticed that if you were extremely nice and overdid things for others, you received more love and appreciation.

**Compliance:** You noticed that you were considered more when you complied with everything others said.

**Dissociation:** You might have learned that, by separating your mind from your body, it became easier to sit and take whatever was being said or done. By going to another place mentally, you did not have to focus on what was happening.

**Negative self-talk:** By speaking to yourself in the same way your parent or caretaker spoke to you, it no longer fazed you to be spoken to in that manner; you took back the control.

You had no choice but to explore ways to not be noticed in order to cope. This way, you did not have to deal with embarrassment and/ or pain. Now, you may or may not be aware of your shame. It is important to recognize what drives your behaviors. If you can name the underlying issue and where it's coming from, you can work on taming it. The first step is awareness. Research has shown that when you experience significant anxiety, you can reduce the intensity by up to 50% by noticing and naming your state.[3] This goes to show you how helpful it is to be able to be mindful of your thoughts and feelings. It also shows you the internal peace of mind that being aware of what you experience brings you.

Shame has led you to feel guilty, confused, unworthy, inadequate, bad, and often embarrassed about incidents that have occurred in your life. When something happens, your first reaction might be to blame yourself, speak in harsh words to yourself, or look for further evidence to prove why you are unworthy. This is how your brain has been trained to react since childhood, which makes sense based on how you grew up. But you now have the opportunity to retrain your

---

3        Bruce Freeman, in the article "Name It to Tame It: Labelling Emotions to Reduce Stress & Anxiety" for OralHealth, discusses the concept of naming emotions as a therapeutic technique coined by Dan Siegel in his book, *The Whole Brain Child* (Random House, 2012).

brain and explore different perspectives. As you read this section, you might feel hopeless or think, *Okay, Kiara. How? Because I've tried...* or *I just truly believe things that happened are my fault.* I want you to know that you can rewire your brain's negative beliefs with more adaptive ones. Right now, you do not have to believe the positive beliefs; you just have to want them badly enough for yourself.

A form of therapy that has forever changed my practice in the way I address shame and traumatic events, as well as help my clients in the rewiring of the brain, is called eye movement desensitization reprocessing (EMDR). EMDR was developed by Francine Shapiro, Ph.D., in 1987 as a natural process to successfully treat post-traumatic stress disorder (PTSD).[4] Through this therapy, I learned that the mind can often heal itself naturally—almost in the same way as the body does. This therapy basically replicates rapid eye movement (REM) sleep, which is when our eyes dart back and forth while we are asleep.[5] During REM sleep, our minds often heal naturally. When we go through unprocessed traumatic experiences, our brains take that information and place it in the limbic system. This unprocessed information is placed "raw," meaning just emotions without words, which is part of the reason we continue to be triggered by situations that make us feel the same emotions we felt during the traumatic events. Often, the event can be forgotten, but the feelings and emotions still live in our bodies through anxiety, anger, panic, or sadness.

Due to the constant pressure society puts on you, shame may show up in a lot of different areas of your life. I want to address three important areas that accompany shame in women: relationship status, motherhood, and staying in a relationship when you are unhappy.

---

4        Mailberger Institute. "How Was EMDR Therapy Discovered?" December 1, 2021, https://maibergerinstitute.com/how-was-emdr-therapy-discovered/.

5        EMDR Institute – Eye Movement Desensitization and Reprocessing Therapy. "What Is EMDR?" June 29, 2020, https://www.emdr.com/what-is-emdr/.

## The shame of singleness

We live in a world that places intense pressure on women to be married. If you are single, this may make you feel as if you are incomplete or like something might be wrong with you because you have not found your person yet. Because there is an expectation that you should have already been married, people may ask, "Is there something wrong? What's going on?" during family gatherings. Due to this constant pressure, you might feel rushed to find your person and marry quickly. If you are married, you might feel like you rushed into your union and are stuck now. Because everyone has put this pressure on you, you might believe that there is something wrong with you; you may think you are unlovable.

If you look back at your childhood experiences and how you grew up, what was the philosophy you learned about adulthood? Did you grow up hearing "grow up, go to school, get married, have kids, and live happily ever after"? Or did you grow up being open to different perspectives about life? Open to numerous possibilities of how your life could turn out? If you experienced shame about not being in a relationship or married, more often than not, there was a lot of pressure on the women in your family to marry early to avoid having to marry single parents. (That's another stigma.)

It is important to realize that everyone's life path is different. You are in charge of your life and how you want to live it. In order to fight off the shame that comes with being single, you must own the fact that you complete yourself. Honestly, there is no one else who can make you feel complete and whole before you do it. No one can give you what you need if you don't give it to yourself first. This is part of the reason why a lot of relationships fail; people depend on their partners to make them happy without realizing that they are not doing anything to make themselves happy. It is not fair to rely on others to give us what we do not give ourselves, and it is a lot of responsibility to place on another person.

If you are single and unsatisfied with your life, explore the areas that would make you feel fulfilled prior to entering a relationship. If you are single because you have decided to work on yourself, then do that with your head held high. Continue to take the time to rebuild a healthy relationship with yourself first. Explore your needs, wants, and desires. Work on setting your boundaries and increase your self-esteem. Don't let the world or other people's lives dictate how your life should look.

## Motherhood

Let's talk about the shame women carry surrounding motherhood. There is a lot of shame that comes with being a mother and the choices mothers make for their children. However, seldom are there conversations about the shame placed on women who choose not to have children. There is even shame about the parenting choices you make that differ from other mother's decisions. So, if you ask me, it's damned if you do and damned if you don't when it comes to motherhood.

If you are not a mother, you might get a barrage of questions from family and friends: When will you become a mom? What are you waiting for? You aren't getting younger, so why haven't you? Answering all these questions can be overwhelming. A part of you may feel like you are okay with the life you are living now, so you do not want to have children. But the other part of you knows that if you were to embrace not being a mother and say that at the dinner table or family gathering, everyone would look at you as if it was the most bizarre thing they'd ever heard a woman say. Then, they would attempt to convince you of the reasons why being a mother is so important, making you feel like you are missing out on the experience. In turn, you might doubt yourself, feel guilty, or think that you are selfish. To avoid all of this, because you have already experienced it, you choose to suppress how you really feel about the topic and just say, "It just has not happened yet" or "I am just focusing on myself."

Only you can decide whether it is best for you to become a mother. No one else has that responsibility. As you know, this book was written to help you to become your authentic self, so I am always going to suggest that you live up to what you want and desire in life. This life is your journey to live, and as you live it, you will find that things will change. You will change and experience different stages of your life. This is what others also have to understand. It is not our job to impose our belief systems and what has worked for us on other people. Everyone has had different experiences that have led them to the decisions they make today, so they must figure out for themselves how they want to live. The reality is, you do not want to bring children into this world out of obligation or because it is "expected" of you as a woman. You want to have children because it is what your *heart* desires.

If you are a mother, you might feel pressured to always make the "right" decisions for your children. Children do not leave the hospital with a manual on how to care for their individual needs. Every child is not the same. If you have multiple children or have been around many different children, you might have realized this. Other mothers tend to offer a lot of unsolicited advice, and even though you might appreciate some of the ones you seek out, it can be frustrating to get counsel that you didn't ask for. In general, mothers try to do the best they can for their children (as they should). Of course, they don't know everything, but this does not give anyone permission to criticize the way you decide to raise your children. You are going to make decisions that are not going to always align with other people's beliefs or values, but that does not mean that your choices are wrong or should be looked down upon.

As a mother, I doubt myself even when I know I am doing the best I can in making decisions about how I raise my children. Yes, I have made numerous mistakes, but I continue learning how to be the best mother I can be for my children. I've dreamed of becoming a mother since a little girl; I always knew I wanted children. I just never realized the enormous amount of internal work that was going to accompany it. Only God knows how much I've had to evolve as a human being to be the mother I am today, however; this a never-ending journey as we recognize the importance of always growing and becoming better versions of ourselves. God also knew I needed my children to grow and change; they've saved me.

Some of us need drastic disruptions in our lives to get things together. At times, when those big disruptions come, you have no idea what to do. You begin to explore what would be best for you under the circumstances and may begin to feel shame because of how the experience occurred. Later, you look at those circumstances and are thankful that they took place. God's timing is perfect, so whenever I question why events happen in my life, I remember that he knows better; the timing is always right. Then, I ask myself what I am supposed to learn from the experience to grow. We often face a lot of barriers as mothers, and we feel helpless, inadequate, and even undeserving at times. However, it is important to realize that every challenge comes with a life lesson. If we reframe the way we question ourselves, we will live happier lives. Moving forward, every time a challenge comes your way, I want you to ask yourself, "What am I supposed to learn from this difficult time?" instead of "Why me again?" I am a firm believer that when obstacles continue to present themselves, we have not learned our lesson. So, always seek self-understanding to learn and move forward.

Motherhood is challenging. There is a lot of screaming and running around, sleepless nights, discomfort, doubts about whether you are doing the right thing, and even more doubts when decisions must be made. You might have a lot of opinionated individuals in your life who do not make these feelings better for you; instead, they make it worse by instilling their own beliefs and judgments into your situation. These people might come into your life to tell you the "right thing to do." Always remember, no one else knows your child better than you do. As a mother of two children with completely different personalities, I have learned to accept that I am going to make many mistakes all the time. Also, I have learned how to be vulnerable with my children and apologize when I make a mistake. I am not always going to have all the answers, and that is okay. However, when I make a decision for my children, it is because I truly believe that it is the best decision to be made. If I discover I made a mistake along the way and it was not the best decision, I own up to it, learn from it, and move on.

Allow yourself to make mistakes. This is another journey you are taking on, and you deserve grace. You will learn along the way. You will become wiser. You will become more aware. But this is your process and no one else's. You deserve to embrace this process with all that accompanies it, positive and negative, in order to learn and grow.

## Staying in a relationship when you are unhappy

Growing up, you might have heard stories about the importance of staying in relationships. You might have also heard "I am staying for the children" or "I have to put up with it because it will get better." Some adults in your life may have stayed in their relationships because they hoped that their partners would change, were more concerned about what people would think, thought their children deserved to live in two-parent homes, or believed women were supposed to put up with abuse or neglect. These underlying thoughts and beliefs, keep you going through life in relationships that lack change, connection, and love. The same issues continue to show up for you, and you see no changes being made. But you get wrapped up with everything else in life, so you have to go on. You continue moving with the flow you have created—with your routines. Finally, your relationship becomes part of the routine; it becomes another task.

You might have also felt pressured by friends to make the relationship work because "it's not that bad." Understand that today's society is "pro-relationship," not "pro-separation." You may feel like you are broken or a failure if you cannot make your relationship work, which is another factor that may hold you back from leaving. You might begin to feel guilty or selfish for even having these thoughts. Instead, you decide to suppress your thoughts and continue living day to day. Well, you are not really living. It's more like you are going through the motions. When you go through the motions, you let the world happen to you, but when you live, you are intentional about your actions, mindful, and in control.

You may ask, "How can I take myself off of autopilot?" Identify your needs in the relationship, then be vulnerable and express them. Actively seek change and explore what you can also work on to improve. If nothing takes place after you have expressed yourself gently and lovingly about what you would like to see change, then it is important to have a talk about whether you both should continue the relationship. Have honest conversations about the separation and its impact on your children (if children are involved). Separating comes with a lot of shame, guilt, embarrassment, and judgment because of the society we live in. However, you deserve to be happy, live up to your truth, and feel fulfilled in every way possible.

## *How to combat feelings of shame:*

1. Challenge negative shame-based beliefs.

2. Attend therapy.

3. Speak to someone you trust.

4. Speak affirmations.

5. Work on knowing your inner child.

# Exercise

How does shame show up for me, and in what areas do I see shame?

_____

_____

What are my thoughts about how I developed shame in childhood?

_____

_____

How do I want to face shame now?

_____

_____

How can I work on addressing shame?

_____

_____

What did I learn about myself in this chapter?

_____

_____

# FOR HIM

*This section is dedicated to all men looking for a deeper understanding.*

Being vulnerable is the new strong.

Note: This section can also pertain to women.

# 5 VULNERABILITY IS HARD

*THE GREATEST LOVE IS THE LOVE THAT CAN SHOW ITS VULNERABILITY.*

Vulnerability is difficult, especially if you were never taught that it is okay to be vulnerable. As you read this chapter, I ask that you try to be open-minded and vulnerable. If you struggle with showing and/or managing your emotions, this chapter is the beginning of you becoming your most-evolved self.

Based on assessments I've conducted while working with men and growing up around many men, I have learned that you often feel misunderstood in many different areas of your life. People may automatically label you as "aggressive," "cold," or "insensitive" to their feelings. When this happens, you might think, *What do you want from me?* or *This is all I can give you.* But as you walk through life, it seems like what you have to offer just might not be enough. This gets frustrating and confusing.

Let's talk about childhood and a few ways that your vulnerability could have been suppressed during the early years of your life. One of the most shared experiences among men is being taught that showing emotions is out of character. As a man, you are always expected to be strong and a protector. This could have shown up by you crying because you felt frustrated, got hurt, or were just sad. In response, you were most likely met with coldness, distance, disgust, or anger by your parents/caretakers. You may have most likely heard someone say, "Men do not cry." Now, imagine how confusing this must be for a child.

When someone cries, they often look for comfort, compassion, or understanding. But this is not what you received, so the more this happened, the more you felt rejected, misunderstood, unwanted, and dismissed for being true to your emotions. Ultimately, you grew up in what mental health professionals call an "emotion-dismissing environment," where your feelings were typically discouraged. You may have been told to "stop crying" or "get over it." Connecting with your own emotions was not allowed or encouraged.

I am always shocked when I hear the phrase "men don't cry" being said to a male child because it means that boys were expected to be men, not boys, at an early age. If this happened to you, I am truly sorry. It is unfortunate that our parents' generation thought this was the best way to develop healthy men. However, it is never too late. If you are reading this book, I am beyond happy that you are looking for ways to learn how to be vulnerable and accept that you deserved more love and understanding in your childhood, as well as understand why it is easier to be cold and distant at times.

As a child, all you wanted was to feel accepted and loved by your parents or caretakers. When showing emotion was not getting you that, you learned to hide how you truly felt. As you became older, you learned to channel sadness into something else—something more "manly." You learned that anger was a more "acceptable" feeling for men to show. In fact, you might have noticed the respect the male figures around you got when they became upset, so you began to adapt that emotion as your coping method.

In contrast, anger may have been an unacceptable emotion for you to show at an early age. "What you gotta be mad about?" you heard your parent say. Then, you started becoming good at turning off your emotions. You might have learned to cope by developing the maladaptive behavior of people-pleasing, which is typically not discussed among men. As a child, you might have learned to redirect your emotions into the emotions of others by ignoring your own feelings and focusing on theirs. You learned that if you complied with your parents' or caretakers' wishes and wants, you would make them "happy" and "satisfied." Also, you learned that by doing this, you were met with positive emotions, happiness, excitement, and appreciation.

It makes total sense. If you learned early on that making others feel good at all costs meant you were going to be met with appreciation, why wouldn't you do that? This becomes an issue when you begin behaving this way at the expense of your own happiness, wants, and desires, which will show up in your relationships. I spoke about women displaying people-pleasing behaviors in chapter three; the same can also show up for men. If your friends were your safe haven or safety net growing up, they accepted you for who you truly were. There is a high chance that you learned to always prioritize your friends' needs, even when you were in a committed relationship. Be mindful of how this may show up for you.

## <u>Exercise</u>

What does being vulnerable mean to me?

_____

_____

What does being vulnerable represent from my perspective?

_____

_____

When I was younger, how was I comforted when I expressed or showed emotions?

_____

_____

What were my parents' or caretakers' typical responses to my emotions?

_____

_____

What emotions did I usually experience in my environment growing up?

_____

_____

Write down times you felt you were loved and respected by your parents/caretakers. What did you have to do to receive love and respect?

_____

_____

How does people-pleasing show up for me? What would I like to change and improve?

_____

_____

Now that you have some insight as to how your emotions were typically shut down, let's learn about how shutting off your emotional being has impacted you.

## Ways suppressed emotions show up

Suppressing your emotions can lead to many different consequences, including mental health issues, as well as depression and anxiety. This contributes to the increase in suicide rates in men. According to Statista, from 1950 to 2018, the death rate of suicide for males was consistently higher than that of females.[6] This suggests that men have been suffering in silence for decades. Additionally, suppressing your emotions also prevents you from recognizing them as you feel them. Since you have been suppressing your emotions for so long, you might find yourself going from zero to one hundred quickly. You might also face difficulties controlling your emotions once they are heightened. This is because you were never taught ways to cope and work through them. You were not taught how to navigate conflict, which did not allow you to develop the necessary skills needed to do so.

Overall, men have learned that emotions are for the "weak," which is why it is difficult for them to recognize or apply the language needed to verbalize how they feel. In order for you to be understood and vocal about your emotions, you must understand that society has put a label on what it means to be vulnerable. Somehow, we have allowed society to decide who can and cannot show emotions. It is important to recognize that displaying emotions is a natural process that all human beings experience.

As an adult, you may face a lot of challenges with tolerating negative emotions. In fact, you might be uncomfortable around people crying or being emotional and want to run away or shut them down. Depending on the circumstances, you might communicate that you do not understand why the other person is crying. You might also

---

6 John Elflien, "Death rate for suicide in the U.S. 1950-2018, by gender." *Statista,* July 1, 2021, https://www.statista.com/statistics/187478/death-rate-from-suicide-in-the-us-by-gender-since-1950/.

believe that there is no point in focusing on negative emotions. This all makes perfect sense; you learned that the "right" way to deal with negative emotions was by ignoring them or shutting them off. You think, *What is the point of crying? What is the point of being sad?* Right now, though, I need to you to reflect on how much of the treatment you received from your parents you have adapted for yourself and others. Remember that we are a result of our past experiences and our history.

Crying is a coping mechanism used by many people. It is common for us, when met with coldness for feeling sad or angry, to internalize that, then treat ourselves the same way moving forward. It is also typical that you will ignore or dismiss other people's emotions if you ignored or dismissed your own. Look within and identify your own patterns of behaviors now in order to make the changes needed to develop more meaningful relationships and connections with others.

# Exercise

How do I feel about emotions?

_____

_____

How do I typically respond to my sadness? How do I respond to
other people's sadness? How did my parents/caretakers respond to
my sadness growing up?

_____

_____

How do I typically respond to my anger? How do I respond to other
people's anger? How did my parents/caretakers respond to my anger
growing up?

_____

_____

How do I respond in uncomfortable situations?

_____

_____

What is my current perspective on being vulnerable and showing
emotion?

_____

_____

What changes would I like to make for myself?

_____

_____

## How being an "emotionless man" shows up in your relationships

According to The Attachment Project, parents who are strict and emotionally distant do not tolerate the expression of feelings and expect their children to be independent and tough.[7] This might have impacted you in developing the avoidant attachment style, which means that you might be independent and even social. You might not rely on others for reassurance and have high self-esteem. However, you might not genuinely feel connected to people not really feel known by the people you have surrounded yourself with. When things begin to become serious or deep, you might become cold and distant. Being vulnerable and letting people into your inner world is hard if you have an avoidant attachment style.

In general, human beings seek love and affection, which provides another level of feeling safe and secure. However, due to our childhood experiences, we might not know how to give the feelings to or receive them from others. In my practice, I've consistently noticed the high expectations placed on males being vulnerable, so I always ask for patience from my female clients. Patience is vital because women expect men to give what they don't know how to nor have the skills to yet. Vulnerability takes time; it takes even more time when you have not allowed yourself to be vulnerable with yourself. Not only have you been hiding that part of yourself from the world, but you have also been hiding it from yourself. This partially explains why you might feel depressed, anxious, unfulfilled, or lonely at times. I no longer want you living life thinking you have to carry the load on your own; today, you have been made aware of it. There are so many ways to work through this, change, and live the life you want. You just have to want it badly.

Now that you have a better understanding of your relationship with emotions. Let's take some time to learn how being unable to express your emotions shows up in your relationships. You may often hear that you are cold, a stone, a robot, and much more. You might not get what else you can do or even have clarity about what is being

---

7        "Avoidant Attachment Style," *The Attachment Project*. Last modified January 25, 2022, https://www.attachmentproject.com/blog/avoidant-attachment-style/.

asked of you. When your partner becomes emotional, it might be uncomfortable for you. In fact, you probably feel like you want to connect with your partner badly, but you have masked all of your emotions with logic. You discuss the topic with facts about what makes sense from a logical perspective, which makes your partner feel emotionally alone and dismissed—like you felt when you were a little boy. The emotional connection and empathy are absent. You both are looking to be understood in different ways, which causes you to continue to miss each other.

Showing vulnerability means taking a risk. In working with my clients, I have realized how scary it is for men to display their pain. It is even harder when they do not have the words to describe their emotions. When men do not have the vocabulary to explain their emotions, they become even more frustrated and misunderstood because they are only working with what they have. Then, they leave the conversation feeling like what they have to offer is not enough.

I want to present you with some scenarios on how being unable to show your emotions impacts you and your relationships negatively.

**Emotional support avoidance:** You grew up having an understanding that a man must provide and be a protector, which meant he must always work. Being the provider you are, you feel you take care of all the necessities in the home for your family. An incident might take place where your partner wanted and needed your support regarding a medical issue. For you, support meant meeting the concrete needs (financial, food, clothing, shelter, etc.). You took care of all the concrete needs and went above and beyond to make sure your partner received the care they needed. You even left work early to ensure you could take your partner to their appointments. However, this was not enough. Despite all your efforts, your partner did not feel satisfied. In fact, your partner complained that you were never home and that it seemed like you didn't care about the pain and discomfort they felt. Your partner felt like you had been more absent than ever when they needed you most.

Now, because you are uncomfortable with negative emotions, it makes sense that you would want to avoid being there for your partner emotionally. Because there is no awareness in your relationship about how you are supporting or of your challenges with emotions, there is no understanding about how you have been showing up, which makes you feel confused and taken advantage of.

Several of my clients have presented with similar issues, so this situation happens in real life. A few of the couples were dealing with going through an abortion. Typically, in these circumstances, the women rely on their partners for decision-making and emotional support. I noticed that a lot of men left it up to the women because their understanding was "this is the right move" or "it is your body." Now, this approach led to issues at times, as the women began to feel emotionally alone in the process. Some women also felt pressured to make a decision alone; they worried they would make the "wrong" decision. I have worked with women who have shared that they decided it was best to have an abortion because they noticed how emotionally distant their partners were and were afraid their partners did not want the child.

Here is a typical conversation that I hear in couple's therapy sessions: "Because of you I had to get an abortion. You were not there for me. You did not want to have the child and put it all on me," the woman would say.

Confused, defensive, and upset because of her words, the woman's partner would reply, "What are you talking about? I was there the entire time! Who took you to appointments? Who made sure you took your medication? I took care of you." The pain was apparent through his anger—pain awoken by sadness and frustration and masked with anger.

The woman would then say, "I just wanted you there emotionally. It felt like you did those things because you had to, not because you really wanted to."

At this point, I typically jump in the conversation because I see the woman is being vulnerable and point out that it is a chance for him to learn to empathize and risk being vulnerable, too. I ask him to empathize, take accountability, and share a little bit about what caring for others looks like to him. As I help them move through the conversation, we learn that he is not good with emotions; he is uncomfortable with seeing the people he loves cry or experience pain. He could not stand watching her during those moments when she was in pain, so he found other things to do to avoid resorting to unhealthy coping methods that he did not want to go back to.

In the situation described, that the man could not verbalize that watching his partner suffer and go through the experience of having an abortion was painful and challenging to him. In turn, she thought he just did not care about what was going on. Communication is key. Once they learned how the other showed up in the situation, they were able to gain more understanding and identify areas needing improvement to move forward.

**Conflict:** You might have a partner who breaks down and cries easily when in conflict. You need to realize that you most likely adapted the same communication style your parents/caretakers used to use (harsh, critical, demanding, etc.). Since we often adopt many things from our parents/caretakers, including communication style, you might find yourself speaking in the second person often and saying things like "you are too sensitive," "no one can ever tell you anything," or "you are exaggerating." These statements are received as judgment and/or criticism. When this shows up in the relationship, it is difficult to listen and not become emotionally overwhelmed.

You might also notice that you become upset and explode when you are triggered during conflict. For example, let's say you have been patient and are aware of your communication and how you come across to others. In this scenario, you listen to your partner and try to understand, but your partner is aggressive in their tone and criticizes you. As a result, your inner child becomes triggered, and you are transported to a moment when your parents/caretakers screamed at you or didn't show an ounce of understanding or compassion. You can no longer tolerate it and become infuriated. You might throw things, slam doors, yell, storm out, use contempt, or stonewall.

Many couples and clients I've worked with to address uncontrolled outbursts share that they try to control themselves but can't seem to be able to. When going back to the man's childhood and how anger was managed at home and in their experiences, I typically hear:

- "There was a lot of violence in my home."
- "My siblings picked on me."
- "I used to be bullied in school."
- "I remember only getting what I wanted when I threw tantrums."
- "When I was angry, I was told I should not be, so I used to play video games to ignore the feeling."
- "When I was angry, I used to get hit, which made me angrier."
- "When I was little, I could only defend myself with words, which is why I verbally attack others now."

Remember that anger is a surface feeling, meaning that there is an underlying feeling that seeks to be fulfilled when we are angry. Our negative and positive feelings are informative if we pay attention to them. You have lived most of your time ignoring those feelings, which resulted in you having superficial relationships and devoting a lot of time to your career and professional development. You have allowed people to be around you, but you have put up an impenetrable wall by not letting them into your inner world. This created separation, causing your relationships to seem superficial or even one-sided at times. They have been because it is uncomfortable allowing yourself to be open and vulnerable. You might even be surprised when you find someone you can be open with—who gets you. When that happens, something might tell you to stop, stay away, and/or sabotage the relationship because "it's too good to be true."

Based on the questions you have answered on page 56, you should have an idea of how your emotions were shown in your environment growing up and how you now respond to different emotions. The first step to making changes is awareness.

*Awareness is key. Now, I will give you two tools to begin taking control of your emotions and identifying what you need.*

**Self-awareness:** Begin by paying attention to your body, thoughts, and feelings. Pay attention to how you speak to yourself. What relationship have you created with yourself? Are you typically demanding or critical of yourself? Remember, the first relationship you want to begin to monitor is the one you have created with yourself because that will inform you about the relationship you create with others, as well as the needs you might be seeking that you do not meet for yourself.

As you begin to name the sensations you are experiencing, begin to reflect on why you feel what you feel and explore your early memories to analyze why these may be triggers.

**Expressing needs:** Begin to explore your needs. For example, I need more understanding or validation when I am speaking. As you do this work, you will continue to realize what you need from yourself and others.

# Vulnerability

What is your current perception of vulnerability?

_____

_____

What changes are you looking to make in your life?

_____

_____

What is your plan to begin making these changes?

_____

_____

What are your fears about the process of being vulnerable?

_____

_____

What challenges do you think you may face?

_____

_____

How are you going to begin allowing yourself to experience your real feelings and emotions?

_____

_____

What type of relationship do you have now with yourself, and what type of relationship do you want to develop?

_____

_____

Write what you have learned about yourself in this chapter.

_____

_____

# Five ways you can begin to work on yourself

- Begin to journal.

- Record your thoughts through voice notes.

- Draw, write a poem, paint, write a song, or do something artistic.

- Identify a trusted friend you can confide in.

- Meditate.

# 6 BEING A MAN

*SOCIETY EXPECTS BOYS TO BEHAVE LIKE MEN, ROBBING THEM FROM THEIR CHILDHOOD.*

You may have been raised by a single mother, were the only boy, or were the eldest child. If any of these is true, you likely had to be the support your mother and sibling(s) needed. Actually, after your dad left, all you heard was "you have to be the man of the house now." If you ask me, that is a lot of responsibility for a young boy. Think back to that time. What thoughts or feelings did you have? I can only imagine the pressure you felt as you tried to understand what it meant to "be a man." You knew, though, that you had no option; you had to become what your mother needed—a protector.

Forget about yourself and being able to enjoy your youth. There was sorrow and pain in your household. So, the least you could do was replace the void that your dad left. However, that became a burdensome task. There were days when your mom was sad. No matter what you did, she was still sad; those days were the hardest for you. Your efforts went unnoticed, and what you did to make her happy was not enough. So you continued to look for ways to overcompensate as the "man of the house." Everything you did to fill the void your father left went unrecognized, so you felt unappreciated and became resentful as a teenager.

As the "man of the house," you took on the roles of mediator and protector, which likely forced you to always speak up and solve problems through tough situations. You might have had to shoulder the heavy feelings that everyone at home experienced while ignoring yours. As you got older, you became more resentful for many reasons. First, you were upset that your father left and forced you to take on his responsibilities. After all, you did not ask for his job, so it did not seem fair. Also, you might have had to give up activities you used to engage in, social groups you belonged to, downtime you had to relax, etc. Perhaps the financial situation changed because there was one less income and your mother struggled to make ends meet, which left you feeling heartbroken. Your resentment could have developed as your mother switched from being the emotionally stable woman she once was when your father was around and turned into someone completely different. In order to form a new meaning of life without your father, she learned to become codependent on you.

Think about your childhood experiences for a second and reflect on being raised by a single mom. I want you to think about the roles you felt responsible for and were probably forced to take on. Now, no one ever spoke about the confusion you may have felt at the time about the expectations placed on you. If you were the eldest child, your role model—the person you probably looked up to—was not the best role model in your eyes. Again, what did it mean to be a "good man"? You probably thought it meant staying, not leaving. But doing that is difficult when you have only witnessed men leave their families.

Let's recap. Your father left the home, so you had to make sure you protected your family. You felt responsible for everyone's well-being and happiness, so you forgot about your own needs. I have noticed that men who grew up in situations like the ones previously mentioned are typically overprotective in their relationships and overshare their opinions. If your understanding of being a "good man" means staying in relationships, you might have stayed in relationships you felt unhappy in and tried your best to make them work, especially if children were involved. You might often feel misunderstood or unheard because you wear your heart on your sleeve. Also, you might consider yourself to be a great communicator because you had to become comfortable using your words and articulating yourself well while growing up. However, being able to articulate yourself well does not mean you have great communication skills during conflict; we will go into that later.

There might have been moments in your childhood when you wished your dad was around. Once he left, things were not the same. The routines, environment, and emotions changed. There was also a state of confusion because children seldom have to think about things not working. Parents typically only share positive stories or talk about happily ever after.

As you became older, conflicts in your own relationships became challenging because you did not learn what a healthy relationship looked like nor witness conflict resolution. You might be labeled as arrogant or a Mr. Know-It-All because you never lose an argument. In your conversations, you often feel like people are disrespecting you if they pose an opposing view to yours. As a result, you might have a difficult time managing disrespect because respect was something you had to earn early on in order to become the man of the house.

I want you to pause and think about your approach when speaking to others. Do you typically give others unsolicited advice? Do you share your opinions about other people's problems even though you were not asked? Is your typical approach to solve problems in situations? If you answered "yes" to any of these questions, it makes sense as this was your approach growing up. You had to solve problems and help your mom move past negative feelings while you suppressed yours. You had to always give others advice, or you might have even become your mother's confidant when your father left. You had to share your opinion often in situations and get a point across to alleviate the situation. Now that you're an adult, you may become overwhelmed when you feel you are not getting through to people or getting your point across. This approach may lead your partner to constantly feel parented by you. Remember, you are not doing any of this intentionally; it is just how your childhood experiences shaped you. You had to find ways to cope with what was going on, so you adapted maladaptive coping skills to survive.

Growing up without a father made you the man you are today. You may be responsible, transparent, caring, and empathetic. You might work to ensure you have meaningful relationships with your own children because of your upbringing. In my work with men who were raised by single mothers, I have witnessed their love and compassion. This makes perfect sense because many of the men had to learn how to manage others' emotions early on. Several of them witnessed their mothers' pain, so learning the cause shaped their perspectives in ways they never imagined. The downfall to this is that these men forgot about their own needs and wants; they were only in tune with the needs of others. If you still struggle with having your needs met, please take some time to explore what your individual needs and wants are in different aspects of your life.

Now what? How can you understand yourself and your behaviors more? The first step is recognizing how your upbringing and father's absence from the home impacted you. You need to honor your emotions and feelings from back then. You had the right to be angry about the situation. You had the right to grieve when your father left. You had the right to be confused about all of it and ask questions. Maybe you could not express all of this then, so you suppressed a lot of different parts of yourself in order to be there for others. First, ask people you trust for feedback on your approach and behavior. This can be helpful on your journey to becoming a better version of yourself. Then, speak with a therapist. Therapy is a great tool of support to help you figure out your patterns of behaviors and work through them to change.

To help you begin to uncover your patterns of behaviors, answer the questions in the following exercise.

# Exercise

How was I impacted after my father left? What impact did my father leaving have on me?

_____

_____

What patterns of behaviors did I incorporate into my relationships due to this experience?

_____

_____

What moments did I wish I could share with my father?

_____

_____

What did I think when my dad left?

_____

_____

What did people around me say when this happened?

_____

_____

How did it impact me? (Answer if you are the youngest or middle child.)

_____

_____

How did becoming a man earlier on in life impact me?

_____

_____

What emotions did I feel when I found out I had to be the man of the house?

_____

_____

What types of trust issues did I develop?

_____

_____

Not having your father around could have taught you that people were unreliable, inconsistent, and prone to abandon others when things became difficult. If your father was a source of fun and happiness in your home, his departure may have hurt you even more. You may have felt like a part of you died when he left. The loss boys experience when their fathers leave is seldom discussed; the pain and grief young men feel is often not even acknowledged. It gets hard and lonely for them. If this was the case for you, you might have walked through life hearing "suck it up," which was yet another reminder that you could not feel your emotions or complain. You just had to keep on moving.

If you were to research "boy growing up without a father," you would find all the horrific impact not having a father in the home can have on men. *In a Perfect World* is a documentary that followed eight single mothers throughout their journeys in raising their sons.[8] These families were all from different backgrounds and cultures, yet filmmakers were able to show how the experience of not having a father made the men more attuned to the types of fathers they wanted to be for their children. Ultimately, the men looked up to and were inspired by their mothers.

Often, we allow statistics to dictate our perception of individuals, but you no longer have to be another statistic in society. Yes, you grew up without your father. Yes, it impacted you in many ways. However, this does not mean that you are powerless in being the father you want to be now; you can be the best version of yourself starting today.

---

8    Daphne McWilliams, *In a Perfect World* (Seventh Child Productions, 2016), *Showtime.*

## Fatherhood - Making your own story

As I watched *In a Perfect World*, I could not stop thinking about my own observations in my practice and in my life. I have been around a lot of single mothers raising boys, and they have done an amazing job. These mothers raised gentlemen who are empathetic and compassionate. However, due to the stigma about fathers and society's expectation that fathers do not stay or do enough, these men are often punished by not being considered as much as women are sometimes. As you read this book, you might be on your own journey to becoming the best father you can be to your children. You might feel alone and even empathize a bit with other fathers who were raised by single mothers. The system is often set up to fail you but do not give up. Even though society has a perception of who you are, your children will know one day how much you fought to be in their lives. They will feel wanted and cared for once they learn all that you did to have more time with them and be involved.

Let me be clear, not all fathers choose to be absent from their children's lives. In some instances, mothers make it challenging for a man to play a role in his children's lives after an unhealthy breakup. I want to bring awareness to how much this impacts young children and the father's journey. If you can relate, please hear me out. Your relationship with your ex was unhealthy. Things did not work with your spouse, so you decided that it was best to move on. However, your ex was resentful about a lot of things you did, whether she expressed them or not, so she decided to take matters into her own hands. Living in a resentful world can be dangerous, but resentment informs us of our needs. In the situation I'm discussing, the resentful feelings are toxic because they are present in your co-parenting relationship; you might feel like you are always being picked apart or things are not being made easier for you to be present in your child's life. You might have gone to court to get visitation rights, but your ex might make it difficult at times just to get a rise out of you. Also, you might feel stuck and on the verge of giving up on the process—not your child—because it is rarely in your favor.

I know several fathers who are absent from their children's lives not by choice but due to co-parenting issues. I can only imagine how frustrating it might be for you to want to see your child but be unable to due to the conflict going on with your ex. When co-parenting becomes difficult or you find it challenging to connect with your child, I always recommend that you seek help. Choose to no longer suppress your thoughts, emotions, and feelings at the expense of your child's well-being. Continue to speak up and share your truth. Participating in therapy is a way to bond with your child and work through co-parenting issues with your ex in order to reach a compromise.

# What more can I do when I have tried everything to be involved?

- Be vulnerable and express that you really want to be part of child's life.

- Seek family counseling to learn ways to co-parent.

- Work as a team for your child.

- Strengthen communication and conflict resolution skills.

- Be understanding and empathetic when having discussions with your ex.

- Seek outside support (i.e., fatherhood groups).

NOTE: There are many benefits of healthy co-parenting for your child. Through co-parenting, your children learn that love and respect go beyond the relationship. Also, they learn that things do not always have to end badly just because a relationship doesn't work out between intimate partners. By watching you and your ex co-parent in a healthy way, your child will learn that their needs and emotions matter, as well as the beauty of what being a team looks like despite any existing differences.

While some men who grew up with their fathers in the home intentionally choose to be active in their children's lives, other men make the opposite decision. Although this choice can be for numerous reasons, the root justification is that it is difficult for some men to be fathers to their children when their fathers were not there for them. If this is true for you, you might even think you are not needed in your child's life or won't do a good job as a father because you don't know what you are supposed to do. You might have tried to be part of your child's life, but it never seemed like what you did was good enough. Honestly, many parents do not know what they are doing when it comes to raising children, but they try to love and provide for them the best they can. If you are absent from your child's life or have chosen not to be as involved due to past traumas, I challenge you to think about what has influenced you to make that decision. What would you have to change or improve about yourself to be more involved?

Your child deserves to have you around. You matter and should be present in your child's life. You are needed. Your perspective, journey, and teachings are all needed. Provide your child with a different view of life and tell them how much you love and want them.

On the next page, I have listed a set of questions for you to work through some of what you just read.

## Exercise

What type of father do I want to be?

_____

_____

What do I love most about being a father?

_____

_____

In what areas do I want to improve?

_____

_____

What has made it challenging for me to be an involved father?

_____

_____

How can I overcome those challenges?

_____

_____

How can I co-parent with my ex as a team for the betterment of our child(ren)?

_____

_____

# 7 THE PUNISHER

*HAVE PEACE WITHIN YOURSELF SO THAT YOU ALWAYS DO THE BEST YOU CAN.*

Growing up, a lot of emphasis might have been placed on your education, the sports you played, or any activity you participated in. Perhaps you only received praises when you did well in some of those areas, but sometimes what you brought to the table was sometimes not quite good enough. There was a lot of criticism, judgment, and high expectations, so you were often told to "try harder." Now, as an adult, you have difficulty being present because you constantly worry about something. You are typically angry, irritable, and stressed out. You have placed on yourself the high expectations your parents put on you, so you seek perfection, which leads you to feeling unsatisfied when things are not done the way you expect them to be done. Others may find the work to be amazing, but you do not. In turn, you punish yourself by robbing yourself of the joy and satisfaction of a job well done. You might be successful in life and have worked hard to get where you are because you learned in childhood that you received love whenever you succeeded. But after you got what you had worked so hard for, you realized that you still felt unsatisfied and empty. Why? Well, emotional connection is one of the most important factors you must also implement in the process, but it has been neglected along the way.

Because of the constant pressure you are under and stressful situations you find yourself in, you might pick up an unhealthy habit to help you cope. For example, you may use substances to cope because it is only in those moments that you feel the pressure is off you. By doing this, you have developed a maladaptive coping system to temporarily feel what you wish to feel when you are sober. Now, how can you live the life you want? How can you take all this pressure off yourself and be free?

The first step is recognizing that you have internalized the demanding voices of your parents or caretakers saying that you must do better or that what you do is not good enough. I am not saying that you cannot have expectations for yourself; you can. But those expectations must be balanced. Putting pressure on yourself and constantly overworking is another way of suppressing your emotions and thoughts. The more we ignore ourselves, the more complicated life can become. It's time for you to connect with your inner self to become who you want to be—who you choose to be.

# Relationships

In your relationships, you may occupy your time with work, resulting in you not "being present" even when you are physically. Imagine how challenging this can be for your partner. It can also be hard to satisfy you because you are not able to relax; it is difficult to have fun with you or be excited about something. In turn, this makes your partner feel alone—like you are unhappy in the relationship and no longer want to be in it. To you, this isn't an issue because you recognize that you have to work, but your partner may view this as them not being good enough or deserving of your time.

I get it. Very little to no attention was placed on your emotions during your childhood, so it makes sense that you have lived your life not paying attention to them either. You learned early on that showing your emotions would not get you anywhere but working hard all the time would. The truth is, you will continue to feel unsatisfied and as though you are hard to please if you do not learn what makes you happy—your needs and desires. No one will be able to satisfy you until you are aware of what you need to be satisfied.

At times, you might come across as being harsh and not understanding. Remember, you have high expectations and might apply those same expectations to others. I wrote this book because you may not even be aware of this about yourself. A lot of times, we treat ourselves the same way we treat others. If you are in a position of power, your staff might feel pressured all the time or feel like they never do good enough work. While you may think you are motivating others to do better and succeed, the recipients of your words and action may end up feeling lonely, unsupported, unworthy, and inadequate.

To identify your patterns of behaviors, here are some questions you can answer.

## Exercise

Am I a "punisher" to myself and others?

_____

_____

How does "punishment" show up for me?

_____

_____

What feedback have I received from others?

_____

_____

What experiences did I have during childhood that led me to develop this behavior?

_____

_____

What do I want to change and/or improve?

_____

_____

What is on my mind when I am spending quality time with family/ friends?

_____

_____

We are our harshest critics, and we live in a world where we are constantly punished for being ourselves, having ideas, and displaying our emotions. We live in a world where perfection is expected. Why add more pressure to avoid the inevitable?

As the "punisher," you might often be really hard on yourself and perhaps others. Paying attention to how you treat yourself and others will support your well-being and the well-being of others. This will help you create meaningful relationships, deeper connections, intimacy, love, and joyful moments, but that can only happen if you stop and listen to yourself. You have lived your life listening to others and following directions. Now, listen to yourself and work through your traumatic experiences. Be kind to yourself in the process.

You get one life, and you deserve to live it to its fullest potential with those you love. If you are a punisher, think about the changes you can make to begin to slow down and smell the flowers along the way.

## Tips to cope

- Meditate to increase mindfulness.

- Request feedback from those you trust to bring self-awareness about your patterns of behaviors.

- Be intentional about how you spend your time.

- Giving yourself grace.

- When mistakes are made; ask yourself, what was I supposed to learn from this experience.

# 8 POWER & CONTROL

*IF EVERYONE TOOK TIME TO SELF-REFLECT, THE WORLD WOULD BE A BETTER PLACE.*

We all have power and control issues. There is a spectrum, of course, like with anything else. Innately, however, we all want to feel powerful in different areas of our lives; we want to feel as though we are in control. If this chapter pertains to you, stay open-minded and take time to genuinely reflect on how power and control show up for you and why.

As a boy, you developed certain beliefs about yourself. You were brought up to see yourself in a different light because you learned that men didn't cry, so you began to avoid your emotions. Also, you were told that certain things—liking the color pink, washing dishes, and taking care of the children and showing them love—were for girls/women. Basically, you were taught that each gender had a set of responsibilities—a specific role to play. As a man, your job was to be in charge and "get things done." As a result, this made you feel like you always had to be in control. If you were not, then you had to do anything to regain power; otherwise, it would be seen as disrespect. This way of raising boys becomes an issue because it teaches them that they cannot be vulnerable; they must always be strong. So, as they get older, they begin to develop resentment because of their life experiences and lose control of their tempers every time something does not go as expected. This can become an abusive pattern, impacting everyone involved.

As an adult, you may now have issues controlling your angry outbursts, or you might become irritated by minor things. You can't seem to understand at times and often feel remorseful about your behavior or the way you expressed yourself. You might often think, *I just don't understand people.* The truth here is, you do not even understand yourself at times. This makes total sense. If you grew up in a violent environment, you might have also learned this behavior because from your abusive father, mother, or caretaker. To you, aggression was the way to resolve issues, so it became your repeated pattern of behavior. The difficulties you might face to understand how to manage the behavior make sense because you were never taught how to do it.

If you were brought up in an environment where love and affection were never shown, you may have only been met with constant anger and abuse. You might have often felt lonely or sad because you were regularly manipulated humiliated, abused, or yelled at. As you grew older, you began to look for things or people that you could control. You might have bullied your younger sibling or other children at school to let out the anger and frustration you kept inside.

Your brain is shaped in the early years of life. According to Child Welfare Information Gateway, "When infants and young children are exposed to chronic or acute maltreatment within the caregiving context, brain development may be compromised and emotional, behavioral, or learning challenges may persist, especially in the absence of targeted and trauma-informed interventions."[9] Understanding your history and traumas give you an opportunity to discover what led you to behave, think, and feel the way you do. Looking back will allow you to further understand your patterns of behaviors, as well as give you the opportunity to grow and change into the best version of yourself. I have worked with many men who had abusive tendencies and struggled with exploring their past traumas because they did not want to cry. Once we unpacked that and explored the meaning of crying, they were able to open up and allow themselves to freely release their emotions. The relief these men felt afterward was amazing. They had been holding all their emotions in with no safe space to let them out, not even with themselves. I challenge you to look within and let

---

9    Child Welfare Information Gateway, "Supporting brain development in traumatized children and youth." *Bulletin for Professionals* (September 2017): 2.

go. You deserve to live a loving life for yourself and others.

As an adult, you might look for love in unhealthy ways. You might look to be satisfied in unhealthy ways to escape reality at times. It might also be hard for you to accept love because that is not something that was ever given or shown to you, so there might be situations that you sabotage for yourself. It's difficult to connect emotionally when being vulnerable and open is something you never learned. However, now you have the opportunity to make the changes needed for yourself. Now you have the opportunity to grow and recognize that your past no longer has control of you or who you are today. You get to make that choice now because everything is a choice.

## How power and control show up in intimate relationships

Power and control show up differently for everyone. As I mentioned before, there is a spectrum. If you are at the lower end of the spectrum, you might become upset, storm out, or raise your voice in certain situations. If you are somewhere in the middle of the spectrum, things might get more intense when you experience conflict, so you might yell, throw things around, become physical by grabbing the person you are speaking with, or use degrading language. Also, it might take some time or be hard for you to calm down. If you are on the higher end of the spectrum, you might become physically or emotionally abusive, seek to instill fear in your partner, or want to control your partner's behaviors, social media usage, finances, etc. These behaviors are considered to be intimate partner violence. It is important to understand where you fall within the spectrum and what is necessary to change. When you possess so much power and control over your partner's world, you create an unhealthy and abusive environment. In turn, your partner grows fearful of you and afraid to be themselves, speak their minds, or open up. This may be the case even if you are on the lower end of the power and control spectrum. If you meet me with anger every time I bring something to your attention, I will no longer feel confident in doing so again, which will result in us growing apart. For the sake of the relationship, it is crucial to seek help—individual help—for support in breaking these patterns of behaviors.

Also, remember that a lot of these behaviors were adapted as a way to survive in your environment growing up. You might have lived your life feeling like you always had to defend and look out for yourself so that you were not taken advantage of. However, you are no longer that child or abused person. Since many of us do to others what was done to us, pay attention to the things you do now to the people you love most because those things were done to you. In sessions, men often stated that their parents never respected their boundaries, showed affection, or spoke to them without yelling. After further assessments and questioning to better understand the situations, I learned that those men behaved the same way whenever they were upset with others. It was not until they were able to make the connections for themselves that they were able to change and move forward.

Men who recognize that they may have anger issues are okay with exploring how they can change and control their anger. The first step is accepting that there is an anger issue that needs to be worked on. Now, take time to answer the following questions about yourself to help you look a little deeper.

# Exercise

Describe the environment you grew up in.

_____

_____

How was love shown to me?

_____

_____

How was anger managed in my home?

_____

_____

How did I begin to take control as I became older?

_____

_____

Where am I on the spectrum of power and control today?

_____

_____

What are some behaviors I want to change?

_____

_____

How motivated am I to make the necessary changes?

_____

_____

Who would I like to include in my healing process for emotional support?

_____

_____

What are my fears about allowing myself to revisit old wounds?

_____

_____

## Tips to cope with anger

1. Explore where you are on the spectrum.

2. Ask people you trust for feedback.

3. Let people close to you join you on your journey.

4. Build a support network (i.e., anger management group).

5. Explore getting therapy.

6. Become aware of your body's reactions when you lose control.

7. Ask for a break when you feel you are becoming upset.

8. Express how you feel.

9. Meditate to increase mindfulness and self-awareness.

10. Learn how anger shows up and your triggers.

11. Be intentional about your process.

12. Be patient.

# FOR THEM

*Love is patient, love is kind. It does not envy, it does not boast, it is not proud. It does not dishonor others, it is not self-seeking, it is not easily angered, it keeps no record of wrongs. Love does not delight in evil but rejoices with the truth. It always protects, always trusts, always hopes, always perseveres.*
*- 1 Corinthians 13:4-7 (NIV)*

Note: This section can also pertain to single individuals.

# 9 LOVENVIRONMENT

*WE ARE SO PREOCCUPIED WITH WHAT A CHILD MIGHT BECOME IN THE FUTURE THAT WE FAIL TO REALIZE THAT HE IS SOMEONE TODAY.*

Love is a deep emotion that many of us want to experience. I have always loved love and have been blessed to be able to experience this feeling in my life. However, the process has not always been easy. I have had to fight and challenge myself in order to experience love. Also, I have had to unpack and unlearn many destructive patterns of behaviors to allow people in. This includes reflecting back on painful childhood experiences to identify what prevented me from connecting and having deep, trusting intimate relationships. I also had to learn to trust others and, most importantly, myself. The first experience we have with love is with our parents or caretakers. For many of us, that relationship was unhealthy, which led us to unhealthy relationships as adults because those "red flags" felt comfortable.

Relationships can be complicated. They all come with a series of unique issues you might have never faced before. However, they tend to lead you to emotions you have felt before, as well as patterns of behaviors from your childhood experiences that you no longer want to repeat. We all grow up in different environments, so the probability is high that love was shown differently in those environments. In some homes, love was shown by being critical and judgmental. In other homes, it was shown by yelling and corporal punishment. Still in other homes, love was shown by providing space to express emotions and hurts; this was met with affection and compassion. What was your home like?

## Exercise

Write down the different ways you were shown affection, love, and care (whether healthy or unhealthy).

_____

_____

What ways have I incorporated into my own relationship (healthy or unhealthy)?

_____

_____

Describe the relationship between your parents/caretakers.

_____

_____

What are the similarities? What are the differences? Also write what you plan to do differently to improve.

_____

_____

How do I currently want to be loved?

_____

_____

If you are in a relationship, how does your partner want to be loved?

_____

_____

If you are in a relationship, please share your answers with your partner to begin strengthening your bond.

_____

_____

By now, you have identified how you were shown love growing up and some things you have adapted from the way you were loved. In the previous chapters, we discussed some maladaptive behaviors that show up in our relationships and why. When we are born, we have many different needs—physical, mental, and emotional—that must be fulfilled. Unfortunately, more often than not, our caretakers do not fulfill all our needs, which causes us to shut down parts of ourselves because we learn that having certain needs is bad or unnecessary. We learn this because those parts of who we are typically get rejected or are met with anger.

Some examples of what you might have experienced as a child and look for in your relationships are the following:

As a child, the only way you got your parent's/caretaker's attention was by throwing a tantrum. As an adult, you continue to look for attention in this way. You might become upset easily and have difficulty self-soothing. When this happens, you may want to know that your partner still loves you no matter what.

As a child, your parents/caretakers only provided you with validation and understanding when you did well in school. Now, you look for validation and love through your achievements.

As a child, you felt abandoned by a parent/caretaker, so you now fear that your partner will leave you at any time, causing you to experience anxiety and even engage in harmful behaviors in the relationship.

As a child, it may not have been acceptable to speak about your feelings, so you struggle with being vulnerable with others and expressing how you feel. You also may experience challenges being affectionate, which disrupts your ability to feel fully connected to others.

You may have been raised by a single mother, so you learned to be an independent woman based on the words you heard your mother say to you or through witnessing her actions. Now, as a woman it is difficult for you to let your partner help or even be part of the decision-making process. You may also fear that your partner will have the upper hand in any situation, so there is a constant tug of war in the relationship.

You may have been raised by a single mother, were the only boy, or were the eldest child. You had to learn how to be the support your mother and sibling(s) needed. As a result, you became a mediator and protector, which likely forced you to always speak and solve problems. Now, you struggle with feeling misunderstood and unheard in your relationship, so you may postpone having certain conversations or insist on solving issues in the moment even when it is not a good idea.

If you grew up in a home without structure as a child, you might have gone out and lost your sense of time when you became a teenager. Since you were never held accountable for your lack of regard for others when going out past your curfew, you now fail to communicate with your partner when your plans change. You tend to live in the moment and not think before you agree to do something different than what was originally planned (people-pleasing tendencies). Lack of structure in the home can make you unaware of time, which may make your partner feel disregarded, disrespected, or unconsidered.

Growing up, your parents/caretakers might have been strict, so you constantly looked for ways to please them. You also began to look for the best in them, at all costs, in order to love them. Now, as an adult, you are a people-pleaser, always looking for the best in people even when they show you their true colors.

Growing up in a household where you were always criticized or praised for your appearance will cause you to become hypercritical about the way you look. This can show up in your relationship as you being unable to accept compliments, which are downplayed or met with a response like "no, I don't look that good." It can also show up as you regularly highlighting how good you look, which may make people perceive you as superficial or arrogant.

Growing up in a household where negative emotions were looked down upon or not shown at all might have made you grow up to think that negative emotions are bad and not supposed to be experienced. These are only a few examples of the different types of environments we can grow up in. It is to provide you with some perspective to begin to identify what your environment was like and how it is impacts you now.

A lot of us grow up believing that love should be easy and smooth. We think it should be a fairytale, and everything should always be magical. The moment you experience anything less than happiness in a relationship, you may begin to think, *Is this even the relationship for me?* or *I do not deserve this*. Love is hard and requires constant work. Think about the early stages of your relationship and what made it easy. Make a note of what you just thought about for later.

Love is a beautiful feeling and, like everything else that makes you feel happy, requires commitment to the work that needs to be put in. Let's say that you have decided to be intimately involved with someone you met a few months or years ago. You spend most of your hours and days with this person who also has their own story, culture, family dynamic, and traumas. Of course, there will be issues in different areas of your relationship. You will not see eye to eye on many topics, but that is the beauty of love: bringing two different people from different walks of life together. Being in a relationship forces you to learn things about yourself that you never knew. Yes, it will be hard at first, but the more you learn about each other's childhoods, the more you begin to understand each other's needs and develop empathy to strengthen the relationship.

Many of us enter relationships as broken people. Even though it is our individual responsibility to heal, it is also nice to have a person who is there to go through the journey with. So how about you help each other create better versions of yourselves? Do it for yourself, your partner, your relationship, and your family.

## Beginning to identify the wounds you are trying to fulfill in your intimate relationship

Below are a few questions for you to dig deeper into how your needs were fulfilled as a child. Try to go back in time and explore what your needs were then.

_____

_____

What needs did you have as a child from your mother, father, caretakers, or siblings that went unfulfilled?

_____

_____

How were you disciplined growing up?

_____

_____

What feelings did you experience repeatedly?

_____

_____

Which parts of yourself did you shut down because you did not feel safe to show them?

_____

_____

What made you feel rejected?

_____

_____

How do you look to fulfill your needs within your relationships?

_____

_____

What triggers you?

_____

_____

What happens now when you are vulnerable in your relationship?

_____

_____

What do you experience? How do you show your vulnerability?

_____

_____

# 10 WHY MARRIAGES FAIL

*SUCCESSFUL LONG-TERM RELATIONSHIPS ARE CREATED THROUGH SMALL WORDS, SMALL GESTURES, AND SMALL ACTS.*

— *JOHN GOTTMAN*

Life happens and time never stops. We are always on the go, working on ourselves, our careers, dreams, desires, hobbies, children, and so on. One of the things we tend to put in the back seat when a lot is going on is our intimate relationship; we stop feeding it. One of the principles Dr. John Gottman speaks about in his book, *The Seven Principles of Marriage*, is the importance of turning toward.[10] So, turning toward your partner is a bid for connection in your relationship, which is extremely important. What does this look like? How would you know your partner is making a bid for a connection? I will answer these questions for you.

A bid for connection is when you or your partner intentionally or unintentionally reach out to one another to connect. There are three ways to respond to your partner's bids for connections: turn toward, turn against, or turn away. Turning toward means you respond to the bid. Turning against means you verbally or physically reject the bid. Turning away means you ignore your partner completely.

Bids for connection can come in different forms. Your partner might try to engage you in watching a show. In response, you might say, "I do not want to watch this," which means you are turning against their

---

10    Gottman, John M. The Seven Principles for Making Marriage Work: New York: Three Rivers Press, 1999.

bid because your partner was looking to connect with you. If you decide to watch the show with your partner but are on your phone, then you are turning away. Finally, if you decide to watch the show and are present with your partner, you are turning toward the bid. A bid could also be something as simple as your partner telling you how beautiful the moon looks. Receiving a one-word response from you lets your partner know you are present.

If you are in a relationship, did you pay attention to the little things when you began dating? You may have been intentional about ensuring you connected all the time with your partner, so you were present. It was hard to miss bids for connections then. However, time passed, and life became busy. In my experience working with couples (and in my own relationship), identifying bids for connections has helped tremendously. Also, expressing when the feeling of rejection came up after a bid for connection was made prevents missing each other. You may make a bid for connection that goes unnoticed by your partner. You may only recognize when this happens after experiencing negative emotions from feeling rejected or ignored. It is our responsibility to acknowledge the missed bid and verbalize how we feel to our partners. Remember, your partner cannot read your mind. As Dr. Gottman's research shows, turning toward is a great indicator of how successful your relationship will be. So have regular conversations with your partner about the things you typically do when you are trying to connect with each other. Bids for connection can easily turn into rituals of connection, which I will speak about later in this chapter. [11]

---

11      John M. Gottman, *Eight Dates: Essential Conversations for a Lifetime of Love* (New York: *Workman Publishing, 2018), 8.*

# Turning toward exercise

What bids for connection do I typically make in my relationship?

_____

_____

How do I try to connect with my partner?

_____

_____

What bids for connection have my partner made in the past week?

_____

_____

What has been my typical response?

_____

_____

What areas do I need to improve to better notice my partner's bids for connection?

_____

_____

How can I be more present and intentional?

_____

_____

## Five factors that contribute to failing marriages:

*Who you are:* No longer feeling known by your partner or feeling like your partner does not care about what is going on with you turns to feeling like you are living with a stranger. One way to keep marriages strong is by ensuring you know your partner's inner world. This is what Dr. Gottman calls "love maps." Remember, your partner should be your best friend—the person you turn to when you are going through stressful situations. Your partner should know your fears, aspirations, and goals. When your love maps are updated regularly, your partner feels known by you. This also means that there is genuine curiosity about knowing your partner's inner world. Updating your love maps can include checking in daily about what is going on in your partner's world, learning their stressors, discovering their goals, identifying changes, etc. This also can become a ritual of connection.

*Emotional distance:* In my work with couples and individuals, clients consistently state that they feel emotionally and physically disconnected from their partners. One partner tends not to know what the other is going through, inside and outside the relationship, which causes feelings of loneliness in the relationship. Failed bids for connection are another way to increase emotional distance in your relationship. For example, if I am rejected every time I attempt to engage you in a conversation, hold you, or do something to connect with you, I will interpret your words or actions as you not wanting to. This is the same for your partner. Feeling lonely and unwanted in a relationship is one of the worst feelings to experience.

*Rituals of connection have stopped:* Dating is vital in a relationship. This is a time when you get to connect emotionally and physically, become attuned to each other's inner worlds, show vulnerability, and update each other about your wants, needs, and desires. In my experience, couples that have disconnected from engaging in rituals of connection decrease their intimacy, which causes them to then disconnect emotionally. Within the relationship, they grow to feel like strangers, preventing them from having deep conversations. Some rituals of connection you can develop in your relationship are:
>    **Greeting each other:** The way you greet your partner in the morning or when they get home from work is extremely important because it is a way to make your partner feel noticed.

**Special occasions:** Create rituals around holidays, birthdays, anniversaries, special dates, etc. to make meaningful connections with your partner.

**Travel:** Plan regular vacations as a family and as a couple.

**Activities:** Choose activities you can do together at home: playing board games, shopping, watching shows or movies, hiking, taking showers together, etc. There are endless ways to connect through activities.

***Your partner feeling like they must mask who they really are:*** The foundation of intimate relationships is friendship ("love maps"), which includes knowing your partner's inner world, desires, stressors, and wants. Feeling like you have a partner you can always lean on for good and bad times is a necessity in the relationship. When your partner shares something personal, be empathetic, not critical or judgmental about the experience shared. If you respond critically, your partner will learn not to let you into their world as much because you will not look at them the same. At this point, your partner will begin to adjust which parts can be shown to you, just like they did growing up. This can become emotionally and physically exhausting.

***Lack of appreciation:*** When words of affirmation are no longer provided, no appreciation is being demonstrated. Showing fondness and admiration of your partner increases the respect and emotional closeness in the relationship. When you do not feel appreciated in managing the different roles you play (even if it is the expectation), you might begin to feel resentful because you are unnoticed or not celebrated.

Now, what can you do to make sure your marriage does not fail? Have conversations about the areas that are not working well and need improvement. On the next page, you will find a set of questions to connect with your partner and continue working toward a healthier relationship.

**These questions will open the door to emotional intimacy, clarity, and closeness.**

What makes you feel lonely in your relationship? When do you feel rejected or unwanted?

_____

_____

What stressors show up for you now?

_____

_____

What is your worst fear?

_____

_____

What makes you feel the most competent?

_____

_____

What are some personal improvements you would like to work toward?

_____

_____

What was one of your best childhood experiences?

_____

_____

# 11 COMMUNICATION

*HUMAN NATURE DICTATES THAT IT IS VIRTUALLY IMPOSSIBLE TO ACCEPT ADVICE FROM SOMEONE UNLESS YOU FEEL THAT THAT PERSON UNDERSTANDS YOU.*

— *JOHN GOTTMAN*

Many people think that communicating is the ability to articulate oneself. Well, yes, that is one part of it. Communication is not easy; it is even more difficult when you were seen, but not heard, as a child. Also, communication can be difficult when you did not have a healthy model of what it looked like growing up. Maybe there were many arguments and screams when discussing conflict. Maybe, because of your experiences growing up, you constantly had to be on the defense (in survival mode) since you always felt attacked. Now, you communicate by putting people down, attacking them with your words, and placing blame. As mentioned in previous chapters, many of us learned to suppress our feelings, resulting in us freezing during conflict, shutting down, or becoming contemptuous. Perhaps no one ever listened to you growing up, so you mostly heard people sharing their own points of view without acknowledging anyone else's. In other words, everyone in the conversation spoke, but no one really listened.

Like many children, you may have been spoken down to when you were younger. Your parents, caretakers, or siblings highlighted your imperfections with the hope that it would cause you to change. Now, you might have not only developed this way of speaking toward yourself but also toward others, whether you are in conflict or not. Appearance was big in my family (it still is). Even though my family had the best intentions when expressing that someone needed to lose weight, they communicated it in a harsh way.

In order for effective communication to take place, there are some essential skills needed. When having communication troubles due to constantly feeling unheard or being interrupted, I always recommend first identifying the speaker and listener in the conversation. I always recommend doing this when you are starting to put the skills into practice in order to minimize misunderstandings. Remember, you are adapting a new way of communicating. It may feel very awkward in the beginning, but almost everything feels awkward when learning something new, right? Specific skills needed for the listener are summarizing, validating, empathizing, and taking accountability. As the speaker, postpone judgment, criticism, contempt, and problem solving.

According to Dr. Gottman's research on predicting divorce, he was able to predict the outcome of a marriage based on the couple's first three minutes of a fifteen-minute conversation.[12] This has a lot to do with how the conversation is initiated. Is the person beginning the conversation by judging and criticizing or by taking responsibility for their own emotions and describing the behavior that is making them feel a certain way instead of assigning a characteristic trait to their partner? It is vital that you describe the situation, not your partner, when having discussions. There must be an understanding that the way we communicate—how we speak—relates to how we have been spoken to growing up. Now, before beginning your journey to learn how to apply these skills in your conversations, please first answer the questions on the next page.

---

12      Carrere, S., and Gottman, J.M., (1999). "Predicting Divorce among Newlyweds from the First Three Minutes of a Marital Conflict Discussion," *Family Process, Vol. 38(3)*, 293-301

## Communication style: What is it? Where did it come from?

How were you spoken to as a child?

_____

_____

Did you feel like your opinions mattered when you were younger?

_____

_____

What happened when you tried sharing your opinions? What feelings accompanied that?

_____

_____

How did you cope as a child?

_____

_____

What did you do with your emotions when you could not express them (i.e., suppress them, scream, become aggressive, shut down)?

_____

_____

How do you express your emotions?

_____

_____

What type of communication style have you adopted from childhood?

_____

_____

What happens to you during conflict? Do you blame others or become critical or judgmental? Do you freeze and become unable to speak? What triggers do you think contribute to this and why? When answering this think about yourself, not others.

_____

_____

Now that you have a better understanding of your communication style and where it came from, you may have had a breakthrough thinking about how you were spoken to and how you speak to others. You should now have insight as to what happens when you become upset. As the speaker, are you critical, judgmental, or contemptuous? As the listener, do you get defensive and stonewall (shut down) or become critical?

Let's begin first by learning about problem solving and its implications in the relationship. In your relationship, you might notice there are times when you want to vent to your partner just to feel better. However, you end up feeling worse. At times, you might even feel confused by the fact that the conversation ended in an argument when all you wanted was a safe space to speak your mind. In many cultures, people are raised to help others fix their problems or at least try to. There are different reasons why we bring this mindset into our relationships without realizing how damaging it can be.

So, what does problem solving look like? Problem solving is when you begin to tell your partner what they should or should not do in the situation they are venting about without permission. When you do this, your partner starts to think that you might feel like they do not know how to handle the situation. In reality, they might already know what to do but just want to vent in the moment because they are frustrated about the matter. I will speak more about postponing problem solving under the listener and speaker skills.

## Skills for the listener
*Listen to understand, not to respond.*

The first skill to learn is summarizing or mirroring. Summarizing means literally repeating what you heard your partner say to you. This skill is meant to ensure you heard what your partner said correctly—that you are both on the same page. While practicing this skill, you must try not to interpret or analyze what your partner tells you. Even though this might sound simple, it is not because it involves you getting out of your inner world and becoming attuned to your partner's inner world. After you have heard your partner's perspective, you then politely repeat what you heard. Ask if you got it right and if there is anything else your partner would like to add to the topic. If your partner says there is nothing else to add, you then ask open-ended questions to deepen your understanding of your partner's point of view on the topic if you need more information to better empathize. Your questions should stem from genuine curiosity about your partner's perspective, not to prove your own point.

You might be wondering what open-ended questions are. Open-ended questions require more than a "yes" or "no" answer. These questions allow the speaker to share more details. We want to stay away from closed-ended questions because they tend to be leading at times or at least perceived as such. Below are some examples of closed-ended and open-ended questions.

| CLOSED-ENDED | OPEN-ENDED QUESTIONS |
|---|---|
| Did you have a good day? <br><br> Do you need something? <br><br> Are you happy? | What was good/exciting/bad about your day today? <br><br> What do you need from outside? <br><br> What makes you happy? |

Postponing problem solving is another skill that is important to master in relationships. As the listener, you might be under the impression that you must provide your opinion on the matter when your partner is venting; many times, this is the wrong assumption. I always recommend that couples I work with ask their partners what type of support they are looking for in the moment. Is your partner looking for just a listening ear, compassion, or support with finding a solution to the issue? If it is the latter, then you can include your opinion and perspective on the matter. But first, you must ask for permission. When you offer your opinion, your partner may begin to feel as if you think they are not capable of solving issues and/or like you think they do not know what to do.

Another important factor is to not side with the enemy. When your partner is complaining about how unfair their friend has been to them, do not try analyzing the event and siding with the friend because this can lead your partner to feeling misunderstood and alone, not heard. Instead, take your partner's side by showing genuine interest in understanding their perspective, expressing empathy and validation, and sharing the same feelings. Later, after you have provided the support needed and your partner no longer feels overwhelmed, you can ask if it's okay to speak about your perception in the situation.

Validating is another important skill that needs to be implemented when listening to your partner's experience. Validating means that you can see your partner's perspective even though you do not agree with it. You may say something like, "I can see how you are viewing the situation based on your experiences and the way you are." Many individuals have trouble validating because they feel that it means agreeing with their partner's perspective despite the way they feel about it. However, this really means that even though you cannot see the situation how your partner sees it, you can absolutely understand why they view it that way.

Another crucial skill is empathizing. Empathizing typically follows validating. Empathizing means that you can see how your partner saw the situation and understand why they felt the way they did. You can relate to their feelings and put yourself in their shoes. Empathizing means that you have gathered enough information to be able to feel the emotions your partner felt.

# Skills for the speaker
## *Speak gently and compassionately so that your partner can listen.*

As the speaker, it is important that you begin the conversation by taking ownership of your emotions. Speak about the situation from your perspective using "I" statements, staying away from criticism and blame. You want to ensure you take responsibility for the emotions you felt in the situation. This is where you want to describe the situation, not your partner. For example, if you became upset about your partner not taking out the garbage the night before, say it just like that and add what you need in terms of moving forward.

I have noticed that many of the couples I work with (and in my own relationship) are quick to criticize others and blame them for their reactions and behaviors. Granted, a lot of other people's behaviors are upsetting and frustrating, but there is a healthy way to communicate frustration without putting people down. Instead of saying, "You are so lazy. Why couldn't you just take out the garbage?" try saying, "It is really frustrating to me when I get home from work and the garbage has not been taken out. I need you to ensure the garbage is out, please." When you assign a negative characteristic to your partner, more often than not, they will become defensive. Also, your definition of "lazy" might not be the same as your partner's. Then, the argument becomes about your partner not being "lazy." Within a matter of minutes or hours, you both forget what the original issue even was.

As the speaker, problem solving can also show up in different ways. For example, in the process of venting, you may jump to trying to fix the issue. Then, when your partner offers their perspective, you begin to feel even more overwhelmed. So, as the speaker, you also must identify what you need in the moment to help you de-escalate. Another way this shows up is by already knowing you wanted to vent and did not need to solve the issue but not communicating this to your partner. You might feel frustrated and overwhelmed because all you wanted to do was vent about a situation that has been upsetting you or maybe even making you feel depressed. Let your partner know what type of support you are looking for prior to beginning the conversation. This way, there is a clear boundary and understanding of your expectations for the conversation.

As the speaker, it is vital that you look within and provide enough information for your partner to understand how their behavior triggered you the way it did. When speaking, I recommend that you go back to your childhood and share about a time when you felt the way you feel in the moment. This will help your partner develop more empathy and understanding as to why their behavior made you feel the way it did. This will also help you both to connect on a deeper level. As you share about your childhood experience, you are also healing; your partner will provide you with empathy, compassion, love, affection, and understanding while you express your hurt—something you perhaps never received during childhood when speaking your mind. This is your opportunity to practice being vulnerable with your partner. If your partner follows the steps on how to be an effective listener, you will feel safe to open up and let them in.

Overall, the listener and speaker have skills to learn and implement to guide a healthy discussion. One last important skill you both must master is the art of negotiating. Negotiating is important to reach a compromise. Once you implement all the skills mentioned and have discussed your perspective in the matter, there has to be a middle ground where you and your partner meet. There is a final decision that needs to be made on how to move forward in a way that makes sense while taking into consideration both perspectives. Reaching a compromise can be challenging, but it must be done. When there is no compromising in a relationship, one person might feel like they always give in while the other person might feel like they always give up.

When in conflict, everyone argues differently. The three styles I have noticed and will address are: the people-pleaser, the avoider, and the argumentative responder. You might be thinking, *What happens during a conflict if I show one of these styles?* Well, let's break them down.

The **people-pleaser:** Because you often try to satisfy others, you might give in to the other person's perception of the situation even though you may have a different opinion during arguments. You also may have a difficult time saying "no" to something you do not agree with. You may attempt to set a boundary, but when the boundary is crossed, you may not stand your ground because you think you might lose the person if you do. You also may feel like you always give in to arguments and that other people always have the upper hand.

**Remedy**: Stand your ground. Do not give in unless it's because you both have shared your perspectives and reached a decision that works best for the both of you. Say "no" when others' requests compromise your values and limitations. Be true to yourself. As I mentioned before, you want to make sure people stay in your life for who you are, not for who you are not. Whoever wants to stay in your life will stay, and those will be the people you develop deep connections with because you do not have to pretend or compromise your autonomy; you can be your authentic self.

The **avoider**: An avoider may appear distant and cold during arguments. You may also build a wall to keep people out. You may feel stuck and unable to speak during arguments. You may at times want to open up but feel like something in your chest just does not allow you to speak. Also, you may feel scared to be vulnerable because your past experiences were traumatic when you let people in or put your wall down. As a result, there are no exceptions now. Avoiders who stonewall (shut down) also do it with the purpose of not escalating the argument because they feel that whatever they might say will be met with more anger, judgment, and/or frustration.

**Remedy:** Begin by expressing what you need during the conversation using positive terms. Setting the foundation of the conversation determines how well it will go. Establish rules and expectations for a safe space to open up. Develop a plan for what you and your partner will do if the conversation begins to feel unsafe or you begin to feel overwhelmed. You can say, "Babe, I have something really important I want to bring to your attention and would love for you to hear me out." After your partner responds, you can say, "I would love to feel understood and validated for how I am seeing things." As the listener, if your partner follows the steps outlined in the previous chapter, the chances are high that the conversation will go well. Finally, if you begin to feel overwhelmed, agree to take a break and set a time to return to the conversation.

The **argumentative responder:** You may feel like you have to fix the issue right then and there. You may even come across as being highly argumentative and have a hard time expressing yourself in a vulnerable way, but you can become confrontational in arguments. A lot of this is due to a fear of abandonment. There is an underlying fear that people will always leave you due to past traumatic experiences. So, in most arguments, you may feel like your partner is going to walk out of your life. As a result, you become invasive and do not provide your partner with the space they need because you think the issue must be resolved right away. When you are dating an avoider, chances are high that you consistently feel alone and abandoned because of how they respond to conflict. At times, they can walk out of the discussion or stonewall, which could trigger your abandonment issues. All you may want in the moment is for your partner to let you know that you are worth staying in the relationship for, but this can be hard to articulate when the way you seek acceptance is by expressing your feelings through anger.

**Remedy**: Identify your underlying fear and explore where it is coming from. Be vulnerable and open with your partner about why it is difficult to cope with their way of handling issues. Express how scary it is when they walk away and that you do not know what is going on in their head and are uncertain about whether they want to stay in the relationship. Explain your reasons for wanting to fix the issue right then and there.

## What happens when you become overwhelmed?

Having difficult conversations and arguments can become frustrating. You may feel like you are just going in circles, and nothing is getting solved. You and your partner leave the conversation feeling angry, lonely, misunderstood, disappointed, deflated, and exhausted. What can you do when the conversation is unfruitful, and you begin to feel overwhelmed? Acknowledge during conversations that you both become defensive and reactive toward one another. After realizing that, you can discuss a plan for how to have an argument or disagreement. Part of your plan must include your individual boundaries.

## Tips for planning how to argue

- No yelling.

- No interrupting the other person.

- Check in with yourself first to explore why you are angry before approaching your partner.

- No degrading language.

- No shutting down.

- Express yourself by using "I" statements followed by your emotions.

- Take accountability for your words or actions.

- Take a time-out in the heat of the moment.

- Avoid purposely trying to have the last word.

Body language plays a vital role during an argument. Be mindful of how your body might be communicating that you are becoming overwhelmed or need a break. Once you feel your heart rate increasing, ask for a break and set a time that you and your partner agree on to continue the discussion. During the break, do something to take your mind off the incident. At times, although you leave the event, ruminating thoughts about the incident can remain on your mind, as well as thoughts of ways to respond to your partner's words. Focusing on this will keep your heart racing and your emotions elevated. Taking a break means looking for ways to get your mind off the situation completely.

### The following exercise will help you uncover ways to support your partner and identify how you can improve.

How do I support my partner when I am going through stressful situations?

_____

_____

How can I improve in the ways I have been supporting my partner?

_____

_____

What can I do differently to ensure I am providing my partner with the support they need?

_____

_____

How can I, as the speaker, ensure I get what I want out of the conversation?

_____

_____

## Skills analysis

What skills am I good at?

_____

_____

What skills do I need to improve?

_____

_____

Why do I have challenges postponing my agenda, and what can I do to improve?

_____

_____

What feedback have I received from my partner about how I come across when I speak to them? What feedback can my partner and I give each other?

_____

_____

How can my partner and I support each other on this new journey of communicating better?

_____

_____

What have I learned about myself and the way I communicate?

_____

_____

# 10 ideas on what to do while taking a break

1. Go for a walk
2. Meditate
3. Speak to a friend
4. Watch a show
5. Journal
6. Listen to music
7. Take a relaxing shower
8. Read
9. Laugh
10. Exercise

**How can I apply these techniques? What other techniques might work best for me?**

# 12 ACCOUNTABILITY

*TAKING RESPONSIBILITY—EVEN FOR A SMALL PART OF THE PROBLEM IN COMMUNICATION— PRESENTS THE OPPORTUNITY FOR GREAT REPAIR.*

*— JOHN M. GOTTMAN*

What is accountability? Accountability is taking responsibility for a behavior and/or action we did that intentionally or unintentionally hurt someone else's feelings. Please read that sentence again. As an individual, you must take accountability. Yes, but you must also follow it with a change of behavior. It is our job to look within and analyze why we do what we do and be intentional about wanting to change the behavior for ourselves and our partners.

As children, many of us did not have the luxury of being apologized to when someone hurt us. In fact, we often were hit, screamed at, spoken down to, and made to feel less than; we never received an apology. Think about that. As children, we were constantly hurt and never ever received an apology for that pain. Oh, and let's not forget that some of us were expected to apologize without even having a clear understanding of what we did because no one explained it to us. So, we felt humiliated and confused while we apologized and took responsibility for something we did not even know or understand. If you ask me, it makes sense why taking accountability as an adult can be challenging.

I see apologizing to others as a healing process for myself and the one(s) receiving the apology. I was never good at apologizing. I was brought up never really receiving an apology for things I witnessed: being hit even when I thought I did not deserve it or being dismissed emotionally. So, as I became older, I learned to go through life not expecting apologies and not giving them. It was not until I learned of all the hurt that I was causing others and actually how unhealthy it was that I decided to look deeper within and change. Oh man, I started sending out so many apology texts to those I cared about. "I am sorry I was so harsh to you when you vented to me," "I am sorry I made you feel less than, then got defensive when you brought it to my attention," "I am sorry I was not there for you," and "I am sorry about what I said that hurt your feelings" were some of the messages I sent to people.

Apologizing took me some time to master. At first, my apologies followed an explanation as to why I did the thing. Every time, I noticed how upset people would become when I tried to explain. Then, I understood that explaining why I did the thing made people feel like I was dismissing how they felt; it made the situation about me instead of them. I realized that I was diverting the situation. That was my aha moment. Then, I learned that I also deserved to be apologized to, so I began to ask that accountability be implemented into conversations whenever I expressed hurts caused by my partner. I did not want explanations; all I wanted was "I am sorry I made you feel this way." The explanation could come later when I sought it, but in the moment, I just wanted to feel safe.

You see, taking accountability is deep because it shows you feel remorse for what you did. It shows that you care about your partner and validate your partner's experience. Taking accountability also shows that you understand the pain you have caused and how it made your partner feel. Accountability and validation go hand in hand. Do you remember the definition of validation? Validation is understanding the other person's experience even when you do not agree with it, and taking accountability is when you take responsibility for what you caused the person to feel even when your action was unintentional. Can you see the similarities? Do you see how both tools can play a huge role in having more effective conversations?

Many couples I work with have trouble taking accountability because, for them, it equates to being humiliated, bowing down, or appearing weak. Remember when I mentioned that a lot of us were asked to apologize for things that were not our faults? Well, in those instances, some of us probably grew up to strongly dislike apologizing. Because your underlying belief about apologies might be negative, you tend to avoid taking accountability. When you are unable to take accountability, you might become defensive, point fingers, and cast blame to avoid taking responsibility for what you did. Because there is a lack of accountability, there is constant friction in your relationship. There is never much understanding and rarely any compromise. We must be careful when we have difficulties taking accountability for our actions and are unaware of it because our partners might feel manipulated or made out to be a villain. This is when you might unintentionally make your partner begin to doubt their own reality. More often than not, when there is a lack of accountability, there is also a lack of validation, empathy, and understanding.

At times, people believe they take accountability for their actions when, in all reality, they do not. This is often not about avoiding accountability but about not really knowing how to effectively communicate. If you have identified that you have trouble taking accountability, then you have taken the first step toward change. The second step is learning how to communicate it. Some of us apologize, then provide an explanation right after the apology. We want to avoid doing that for the reasons I explained earlier. Instead, stay in your partner's world and seek further understanding about what you can do moving forward to ensure you do not hurt your partner again by asking open-ended questions. You can say, "I am sorry I hurt your feelings when I stormed out. What can we do next time to make sure this does not happen again?"

While some people struggle with apologies, others grow up being able to apologize, but their behavior does not change. These individuals tend to apologize repeatedly, but it is because they experienced similar events in their lives growing up. They either witnessed it through their parent's relationships, or they were given empty apologies themselves. "False promises" is what I call them. Now, these people have difficulty holding themselves accountable to make the changes they know they need to. If this pertains to you, it can be draining for your partner because, by not changing your behavior, you consistently cause your partner pain and disturb their peace. Try to relate to that. As you become older, you start to realize that you no longer want to be involved in relationships that disturb your peace because you begin to value your sanity and stability. At times, you might find that, when your peaceful state of mind is disturbed by the same repeated action, you feel like "I am sorry" no longer serves you.

# Accountability exercise
## *Ways to apologize*

"I am sorry you felt some type of way when I said the truth."
Incorrect way

"I am sorry I hurt you when I said you were lazy."
Correct way

In the first example, the person was blamed for feeling how they felt. On top of that, the person continues to be insulted. In the second example, the speaker takes accountability for the pain caused and for what was said.

### *Practice apologizing below*

Think of situations in the past that you could apologize for. Practice by starting with these phrases.

I am sorry I . . .

I take full responsibility for making you feel . . .

I apologize for . . .

# Questions on accountability

What did I learn about the way I take accountability?

_____

_____

How was I apologized to as a child?

_____

_____

What has been my experience in being apologized to in my relationship?

_____

_____

What feedback have I received from my partner about how I take accountability?

_____

_____

How do I say "sorry" when I do something that hurts my partner?

_____

_____

What did I learn about myself from reading this chapter?

_____

_____

# Helping Hand

So, when is it enough? This is a question I am asked often. Only you have the answer based on your boundaries, values, morals, lifestyle, and level of peace. Enough is when you decide that you have tried everything and given it your all but, nothing seems to change. Enough is when you both have worked through it all individually and together, but the same issue continues to come up even though years have passed by. There is no expiration date or time frame for when enough is enough; you just feel it.

A lot of couples come to see me when they are barely holding on to one string. They come feeling highly discouraged, overwhelmed, hurt, traumatized, and desperate; they want a quick fix. Some couples never go to therapy because they do not believe in sharing their lives with another person or do not think that they can be helped.

Recognize that there are patterns of behaviors within your relationship that can be difficult to see on your own, so having an expert help you identify and learn how to work through challenging areas them can be beneficial and prevent issues from escalating in the future. The purpose of couple's therapy is to support you and your intimate partner as you obtain more clarity about the issues you are facing and gain skills to better navigate those challenges in life. Therapy is not only for when challenges are being faced; therapy is also intended to explore potential issues that might come up in the future in order to learn the necessary skills to navigate them when they arise.

Meet your partner where they are. If your partner is reluctant to attend therapy, explore their reasons, without judgment, through open-ended questions. Find out their potential fears about attending therapy You might be surprised to learn that your partner is just not ready to talk about their past experiences. Or your partner might be afraid therapy will bring things up that would make the two of you begin to have more issues. Or you partner may be afraid that your relationship is not going to work after therapy. If that happens, then what? Maybe your partner does not feel safe enough to speak their mind. In this case, support your partner, validate their feelings, be vulnerable, and ask if they would like you to share your reasons for why the two of you should go to therapy.

Many people in healthy relationships engage in couple's therapy to maintain their love, connection, intimacy, and bond. However, there are also people in healthy relationships who do not find value in therapy. So, what can healthy couples benefit from the process? They can learn more about each other in ways they may have never explored before. They can learn what has made their relationship last, as well as gain a clearer understanding of the specific ways they fulfill each other physically, emotionally, and mentally. Also, they will be able to explore challenges they might face in the future in other areas of their relationship. There are so many different aspects that build a relationship, including religion, parenthood, values and goals, hobbies, ways of connecting, financial responsibilities, and ways of managing distressing events. Finally, couples will be able to have conversations that they perhaps do not regularly have because of their busy schedules.

As I spoke one day with my husband about our childhoods, traumatic experiences, and how hard we can be toward ourselves at times, he said, "We are all a beautiful painted picture of all of our traumas." When he said that, I could not get the sentence out of my head. I mean, I could not have summed it up better. All these experiences have made us who we are today, and even though there are ugly sides to who we are at times, those sides inform us so much about what we need to evolve into what we want to be.

We all come to this world wanting to love and feel loved. We seek ways to feel fulfilled and full of life. Some of us struggle to experience love or even allow ourselves to experience it. As you age and walk through life, you begin to realize that something must change—something is not okay. But you cannot pinpoint what that "something" is. That is because you must be the one to change and decide how you want to live your life. You are the one who must decide what values and expectations you will have for yourself and others. What are you not willing to put with? Set your limits.

Now, name and write what you want. What do you want out of life? Out of your relationships with others? Out of your relationship with yourself? Today, you have the choice to make your life what you want it to be. You now have tools and an awareness you may not have had before. What changes can you begin to implement today? You deserve everything you want in life. Anything is possible. Our biggest roadblocks in life are ourselves and our limiting beliefs. But those negative beliefs do not define who we are. Those negative and destructive thoughts are not who we are; they have been created and developed from negative experiences we have gone through. We had no control over what happened to us, and what happened to us does not define us. We now get to define who we are and who we want to be every day. Never stop BECOMING A KNEW YOU!

So, I will leave you with this last question.

WHO DO YOU WANT TO BECOME?

# References

"Avoidant Attachment Style: Causes and Symptoms." *The Attachment Project.* Last modified January 25, 2022.

Blum, Sam. "The Five Types of Personal Boundaries (and How to Set Them)." Lifehacker. Last modified July 23, 2021. https://lifehacker.com/the-five-types-of-personal-boundaries-and-how-to-set-t-1847349639.

Carrere, S., and Gottman, J.M., (1999). "Predicting Divorce among Newlyweds from the First Three Minutes of a Marital Conflict Discussion," *Family Process, Vol. 38(3),* 293-301.

25 CBT techniques and worksheets for cognitive behavioral therapy. PositivePsychology.com. (2022, January 26), from https://positivepsychology.com/cbt-cognitive-behavioral-therapy-techniques-worksheets/

Child Welfare Information Gateway. "Supporting brain development in traumatized children and youth." *Bulletin for Professionals* (September 2017): 1-12, https://www.childwelfare.gov/pupdfs/braindtrauma.pdf.

EMDR Institute – Eye Movement Desensitization and Reprocessing Therapy. "What Is EMDR?" June 29, 2020, https://www.emdr.com/what-is-emdr/.

Freeman, Bruce. "Name It to Tame It: Labelling Emotions to Reduce Stress & Anxiety." *Oralhealth* (May 3, 2021), https://www.oralhealthgroup.com/features/name-it-to-tame-it-labelling-emotions-to-reduce-stress-anxiety.

Gottman, John M. *Eight Dates: Essential Conversations for a Lifetime of Love.* New York: Workman Publishing, 2018.

Gottman, John M. *The Seven Principles for Making Marriage Work.* New York: Three Rivers Press, 1999.

Mailberger Institute, "How Was EMDR Therapy Discovered?" (December 1, 2021), https://maibergerinstitute.com/how-was-emdr-therapy-discovered/.

McWilliams, Daphne, dir. *In a Perfect World.* 2015; New York, USA: Seventh Child Productions, 2016. *Showtime.*

Siegel, D. J., & Bryson, P. H. D. T. P. *The Whole-Brain Child.* New York: Random House, 2012.

# KIARA LUNA, LMHC

At times, you might not feel confident enough to open up in your intimate relationships and not know why. Kiara teaches couples why emotional safety is important, the implications of not having trust, and the steps for building emotional safety. The Emotional Safety Master Builder therapeutic package is a 12-week program to help you identify areas that you need to improve in and develop the necessary skills to build emotional safety. By joining the Emotional Safety Master Builder program, you will:

1. Identify triggers in relationships
2. Learn how to cope with triggers
3. Take accountability
4. Be able to recognize patterns of behaviors during conflicts
5. Learn attachment styles
6. Discover maladaptive behaviors developed during childhood
7. Increase individual self-awareness
8. Learn how to cope with triggers
9. Improve communication skills

**Visit knewyoupsychotherapy.com to schedule your free consultation today!**

 @mrskiaraluna

# ABOUT THE AUTHOR

Kiara Luna is a bilingual, licensed mental health therapist and the owner of Knew You Psychotherapy. With over a decade of experience, Kiara has helped couples develop new rituals of connection, increase fondness and admiration, develop healthier ways to communicate, nurture emotional safety, increase intimacy, and develop a deeper understanding of how childhood traumas show up in their relationships. Kiara has been featured in Fatherly, Psych Central, *Bustle*, WeddingWire, and more. As a therapist and powerful speaker, she has been able to help many find their voices and inspire them to grow in areas they never thought they could. Kiara loves having opportunities to empower, educate, and motivate audiences to achieve personal growth through captivating stories and knowledgeable insight.

Made in the USA
Middletown, DE
03 April 2022

63564156R00077